THE DAILY SEVEN

THE SECRET TO LIVING A LIFE OF BALANCED EXCELLENCE

DAVID FABRICIUS

Evergreen
PRESS

The Daily Seven
by David Fabricius

ISBN 1-58169-193-9
For Worldwide Distribution
Printed in the U.S.A.

Evergreen Press
P.O. Box 191540 • Mobile, AL 36619
800-367-8203

DISCLAIMER

This publication is intended for informational purposes only. It is sold with the explicit understanding that the author and publisher are not engaged in providing spiritual, legal, accounting, financial, medical or other kinds of professional advice. The reader is advised to seek appropriately qualified and licensed professional advice before integrating any of the suggestions contained herein.

The author and publisher specifically and explicitly disclaim all liability and responsibility for any liability, loss, injury or disappointment, be it personal or otherwise, that is incurred as a result of the direct or indirect use or application of any information contained in this work.

TABLE OF CONTENTS

PART TWO—PROFIT IN EXCELLENCE

ACKNOWLEDGMENTS

It is with deep gratitude that I thank God for giving THE DAILY SEVEN to me and for the blessing of sharing it with people worldwide.

A heartfelt thanks to Raymonde Koper, Johan Sturm, John Martini, Billy Haws, Mark Layton, Dotti Walters and Michelle Lemmons, for helping me to get started in the USA, and to Steve Harvey, Dr. Tzvi Pearlstein, Wade Thomas and Susie Levan for caring, friendship and help and Mark Layton for early day encouragement. May your lives always be as rich, warm and loving as you make it for others and may your income, peace, joy and satisfaction increase everyday.

A special thank you to Raymonde Koper and Richard Marcotullio for their efforts and help with this book.

Special gratitude to all my dear friends who I have met through my worldwide presentations for YPO and my inspirational role models for The Daily Seven: Karan Billimoria, Jost Hellmann, Fayzel El Kahil and others.

And finally to all the great authors that have gone before me for their fine example—Dr. Norman Vincent Peale, Jim Rohn, Zig Ziglar and all the many others who positively influenced my life and work.

INTRODUCTION

As you read my words, you may be under a lot of stress and pressure and looking for a way to rebalance and restore your life. Perhaps, in spite of all your great successes, conquests and achievements, you are yearning for more purpose, meaning and significance, or better health and more time with your loved ones. You may be wondering what to do with the rest of your life, or what the highest and best use of your life may be. If any of the above describes you, THE DAILY SEVEN can help you.

In your pursuit of success, as defined by the world, be mindful not to lose what money cannot buy—your family's love, respect and presence, your health, and your soul. It is so easy in our pursuit of the latest, biggest, best and fastest, to work longer and longer hours, returning home later and later, and traveling more and more to obtain a higher standard of living. High achievement men and woman are the ones who raise the bar and thrive on meeting great challenges, completing demanding projects, and finding fulfillment in taking great care of every aspect of their teams' projects. Unfortunately, in the process, they begin to neglect their most important relationships and their personal happiness. They set aside non-work related personal development, hobbies, leisure, adventure, and time with their families even though they are activities that center, revitalize and balance them.

I want you to know that I care about you and feel a passionate burden to help you in any way I can. In the pages of THE DAILY SEVEN, I will try to help you create that elusive balance so you can enjoy a life that matters and deeply satisfies. From time to time, I will invite you to take the scenic route to the top of your own success mountain. I will encourage you to take your loved ones with you and go at a pace they can easily keep, because on the extreme routes you may lose them. For a few months, I had the incredible privilege of living in Boulder, Colorado, and traveling in the majestic Rocky Mountains nearby. There I learned the invaluable lesson that if you take a path that never exceeds a seven degree climb, you can reach the peak of a 14,000 foot mountain, such as Pike's Peak, safer and quicker with others than you can by taking an extreme route all by yourself.

Most of my life has been one of extremes—extreme adventures, extreme risks, extreme successes, and yes, extreme failures. That is what it took for me to learn the need for a more balanced life, and maybe it is what you, too, have experienced. Pain is the ultimate teacher; it is the catalyst for all long-term and significant human change and growth. Pain can be the crucible in which your greatest insight, message and contribution will be born. Life is a constant ebb and flow of pain and pleasure and is filled with learning experiences especially for the sincere seeker.

Today I continue to live THE DAILY SEVEN as best I can, but with a much greater commitment, honesty and sincerity than ever before. There are still days when I fail to achieve all seven, but these days are becoming less frequent, and each morning I wake up with a renewed will to do them.

There will be days when on long international flights or due to unexpected occurrences or fate you will not be able to follow THE DAILY SEVEN. If this is only occasionally, that is fine. As long as each day you make a sincere effort and succeed more days than you fail, you will benefit immensely on multiple levels. You will discover that the power of THE DAILY SEVEN is generated by the synergy between all seven of these areas when each is adequately followed over a long period of time.

Ultimately, since all problems have a spiritual solution, this book is meant to be a spiritual bridge that encourages you to cross over into a more balanced life. May it be the breakthrough solution you are looking for and help you to fully understand what truly matters most in life. May it help you know with certainty what and who you truly are and why you are really here.

I do not have, or claim to have, it all perfectly together or to know it all. In spite of my many past God-given successes, I have many failures and weaknesses and rely totally on God for my future, knowing God loves to use unknown, weak and even foolish people to show His might and power.

It is as we recognize and admit our fears, weaknesses, inadequacies and failures that we open the door for God to work His miracles in us for His purposes. It is at this time when the power, love, grace and goodness of God can work in and through us and create a great testimony forged out of our pain. We can become a great inspiration to others as they see how God uses us in spite of our failures and weaknesses. When people see the transformation God has worked in our hearts and lives, they will receive hope and feel compelled to learn and experience how God can transform them and give them the same joy, peace and fulfillment.

After you read this book, it is my desire that you will know your purpose and be able to pray for, love, share with, serve, worship with, fellowship with, and teach others in your sphere of influence about a personal relationship with God and how to overcome daily struggles. You will become relevant in their lives, feel valuable and be dynamically alive. You will experience joy, significance and the authentic fulfillment you are seeking. There is pain ahead, and although it is necessary, you will get through it and find great peace and joy waiting for you just a little beyond that pain. Know that the refining fires of life are necessary, and that the greater your pain—past, present or future—the greater the work that awaits you and the more power your testimony will have to touch the lives of many others.

THE DAILY SEVEN Quick Assessment Test

This personal assessment will enable you to discover where you stand in living THE DAILY SEVEN and help you pinpoint areas you may want to focus on to restore the balance in your life as you reach for higher levels of excellence. To have it all and not lose it all, you have to consistently do it all.

Please read each statement carefully, and circle the number between 0 and 10 that best represents your current level of performance in each of the areas, with 0 being totally neglected and 10 being consistently excellent. Total each section's points and then plot it on the grid that follows. Discover how you stack up, and be better prepared to get the most benefit from *The Daily Seven.*

1. TIME WITH GOD

1. I begin each day with very meaningful personal time with God. 0 1 2 3 4 5 6 7 8 9 10
2. I am in the habit of saying little prayers of gratitude during the day. 0 1 2 3 4 5 6 7 8 9 10
3. I end each day with prayerful time with God.
0 1 2 3 4 5 6 7 8 9 10
4. I ask God to guide me in my decisions throughout the day. 0 1 2 3 4 5 6 7 8 9 10
5. I daily study the Word of God and am committed to living it and sharing it respectfully with others.
0 1 2 3 4 5 6 7 8 9 10

TOTAL POINTS ____________

2. MENTAL DEVELOPMENT

1. I read inspirational, wisdom and/or business how-to or similar books daily. 0 1 2 3 4 5 6 7 8 9 10
2. I make notes as I read and reflect on the best ideas and strategies after reading it. 0 1 2 3 4 5 6 7 8 9 10
3. I immediately implement the best ideas and teach them to others. 0 1 2 3 4 5 6 7 8 9 10
4. I visualize, goal-set, plan and prayerfully ask for the things I want. 0 1 2 3 4 5 6 7 8 9 10
5. I journal, write creatively and seek good counsel.
0 1 2 3 4 5 6 7 8 9 10

TOTAL POINTS ___________

3. PHYSICAL CONDITIONING

1. I work out 6 days per week, no excuses, no exceptions.
0 1 2 3 4 5 6 7 8 9 10
2. I exercise all areas of my body.
0 1 2 3 4 5 6 7 8 9 10
3. I alternate resistance training with cardiovascular conditioning. 0 1 2 3 4 5 6 7 8 9 10
4. I exercise for at least 30 minutes each day.
0 1 2 3 4 5 6 7 8 9 10
5. I stay in the habit of exercising even when I travel and plan ahead for success in this area.
0 1 2 3 4 5 6 7 8 9 10

TOTAL POINTS ___________

4. INTELLIGENT NUTRITION

1. I enjoy a great variety of fruits, vegetables, grains, meats and other sources of nutrition.
0 1 2 3 4 5 6 7 8 9 10
2. I always eat in moderation and watch my portion-sizes carefully. 0 1 2 3 4 5 6 7 8 9 10
3. I ensure balance among the proteins, carbohydrates and

essential fats that I consume. 0 1 2 3 4 5 6 7 8 9 10
4. I drink an ounce of water per pound of bodyweight daily.
0 1 2 3 4 5 6 7 8 9 10
5. I take appropriate supplements for my body.
0 1 2 3 4 5 6 7 8 9 10

TOTAL POINTS __________

5. PURPOSE FULFILLMENT

1. I know the purpose for my life and live it fully.
0 1 2 3 4 5 6 7 8 9 10
2. I have a deep sense of meaning in my life and feel fulfilled. 0 1 2 3 4 5 6 7 8 9 10
3. I can get myself and others to take consistent action, and do so daily with passion. 0 1 2 3 4 5 6 7 8 9 10
4. I express my talents creatively to create profound value for others. 0 1 2 3 4 5 6 7 8 9 10
5. I positively and actively influence the culture, market share growth and revenue of my organization.
0 1 2 3 4 5 6 7 8 9 10

TOTAL POINTS __________

6. FAMILY TIME

1. Daily family time together at dinner and afterwards are totally non-negotiable to me. 0 1 2 3 4 5 6 7 8 9 10
2. One entire evening from sunset onwards a week is totally dedicated to my family. 0 1 2 3 4 5 6 7 8 9 10
3. At least one entire day per weekend is always invested in family time together. 0 1 2 3 4 5 6 7 8 9 10
4. I often give hugs, smile and say sincerely "I love you."
0 1 2 3 4 5 6 7 8 9 10
5. I edify, support and encourage everyone in my family with love, respect and care. 0 1 2 3 4 5 6 7 8 9 10

TOTAL POINTS __________

7. PERSONAL QUIET TIME

1. Every night I take at least 30 minutes to be totally quiet and still. 0 1 2 3 4 5 6 7 8 9 10

2. I have a personal evening quiet time ritual that is 100% non-negotiable. 0 1 2 3 4 5 6 7 8 9 10

3. Periodically, I take time out to retreat into silence for a day or more to renew myself. 0 1 2 3 4 5 6 7 8 9 10

4. I take time out daily to pray. 0 1 2 3 4 5 6 7 8 9 10

5. I go for quiet walks. 0 1 2 3 4 5 6 7 8 9 10

TOTAL POINTS ___________

Total your points in each area of THE DAILY SEVEN and plot each total in the grid below. The higher you place in each area, the better you are doing. The areas with low totals are personal challenge areas that your need attention to create meaningful improvement and balance in your life.

SELF-ASSESSMENT CHART

	1	2	3	4	5	6	7
50							
45							
40							
35							
30							
25							
20							
15							
10							
5							

Where Do You Stand?

Please take some time right now to think about what the results reveal. Your life today is an accurate reflection of your previous thinking and the quality of your past and current actions. As you read each section of this book, you will learn how to strengthen the areas in which you are weak by creating an action plan for improvement. As you cultivate the daily disciplines that are required, you will establish the balanced excellence, the spiritual maturity and fulfillment, the good family life, the improved relationships, the outstanding health, the improved business, and the financial abundance you desire. Decide today to build a better future by using the following proven system to create your own specific plan.

Study the following chapters and apply the foundational building blocks that can create the beautiful life of your dreams. Become the better citizen, parent, spouse, leader, sales professional and friend that attracts greater opportunities and like-minded people into your life.

THE DAILY SEVEN is your key to accomplishing all that. Embrace these seven areas with more diligence and more disciplined growth and effort. They can help you obtain all you ever wanted without losing everything you value. It is time to be more productive and fruitful in *every* vital area of your life by creating more balanced excellence.

THE DAILY SEVEN SUMMARY

The secret to success is to divide each day into seven time allocations to focus on each of the seven areas of THE DAILY SEVEN as demonstrated on the next page. Decide what time you will begin and end each main area and exactly what the highest and best use of your time in that area will be. Know what counts most in your life right now and what will give you the greatest yield for your time invested. For example, take the area of Purpose Fulfillment. Decide how you can best divide an 8 to 12 hour workday for optimum yield. What God-honoring and money-making activities do you need to focus on, and in what order and sequence, to meet your goals?

Schedule your days, hour by hour for each week in advance, find a plan that works best for you and be consistent in carrying it out. Be willing to occasionally break the routine for a day or two, but not for too long, because you never want to fall out of practice. Once your schedule is fully established, you will reap an abundance of good fruits from it, season after season.

THE DAILY SEVEN

The Secret to Living a Life of Balanced Excellence

1. CALL OF DESTINY 5:00 am
   (Daily, Scheduled Spiritual Enrichment)

- Study of wisdom literature
- Prayer
- Spiritual journaling

2. THE DEVELOPED MIND 5:30 am
   (Daily, Scheduled Mental Enrichment)

- Reading life, health, finance & business books
- Knowledge journaling & creative writing

3. THE PHYSICALLY CONDITIONED BODY 6:00 am
   (Daily, Scheduled Physical Enrichment)

- Stretching and breathing exercises
- Strength training
- Walking

4. INTELLIGENT NUTRITION
   7:00, 10:00, 12:30, 3:00, 7:00, 9:00
   (Daily, Scheduled Portion-Controlled Nutrition)

- Optimum hydration
- Optimum nutrition: both balanced whole foods and appropriate supplements

5. THE JOY OF SERVICE
7:45 am – 5:30 pm
(Daily, Scheduled Purpose Fulfillment)

- Using your gifts to fulfill your purpose
- Wise time and resource management
- Sharing with those in need

6. SHARING OURSELVES WITH FAMILY
7:00 pm – 9:00 pm
(Daily, Scheduled Family Time)

- Non-negotiable daily family meal
- Teach godly wisdom
- Spend time on family projects

7. FILLING THE WELL
9:00 pm – 10:00 pm
(Daily, Scheduled Personal Time)

- Quiet time alone
- Spiritual and reflective journaling
- Time of prayer

PART ONE

THE DAILY SEVEN

Practice these
seven daily choices and
bring more balance, relational
happiness, personal health,
financial prosperity, and
spiritual growth
into your life.

Chapter 1

Call of Destiny

Daily, Scheduled Spiritual Enrichment

Truly successful people know that total success includes a happy family, great health, and spiritual maturity. There exists a definite long-term relationship between all the vital aspects of a great life—spiritual, emotional, physical, intellectual and financial.

In my work with business and community leaders, top sales professionals, entrepreneurs and investors from more than 130 nations on five continents, I see the same problem and hear the same question: “How can I build an increasingly profitable business/career without sacrificing my family, health or soul?”

Most of us talk about our need for greater balance but struggle to implement it in our own lives. We are typically people who dream really big and work to live up to it. We often suffer from high blood pressure and are mired in family issues. The most successful among us who are in business wish we could be as successful in our family life as we are in our business life. We want more time with our kids, and we desire to flourish in the spiritual side of our lives, but the truth is that our business projects consume most of our time.

I know what it is like to travel and sleep in one lonely hotel room after another. I, too, have struggled to maintain my exercise plan when I travel. I have also seen how difficult it is for working moms, and, even more so, single working moms to balance their work and their life with their husbands and/or children.

Although the rewards of a busy career are great, I decided that there must be a way to have a more rounded life. All across the world, people are increasingly recognizing the fact that to be a great leader, parent, sales professional or anything else worth being, one must first be a great person. In one country after another, I began to observe how people are searching for long-term answers to help them balance their professional, family, community and personal life.

In my interaction with the top 3% of corporate and entrepreneurial business achievers worldwide, I noticed most of them sooner or later struggle with the same thing that was challenging me. The character trait that makes us so effective and successful—our intense, passionate, and single-minded focus—is also eventually what most threatens to destroy at least two of our most precious gifts and assets—our family and our health.

In the process of becoming an internationally successful business motivational speaker and executive coach, I caused much damage to my own beloved family and even my health—the very things I wanted to avoid. To me this was not acceptable. I began looking for a doable, dependable, and enduring solution. After many years, my eyes of understanding were enlightened. In that quiet and emptiness that only comes to those who have become desperate for answers, I began to see a simple plan—THE DAILY SEVEN. And, along with it, came the compassion, wisdom, and understanding necessary to not only implement it in my own life but also to teach the seven principles to others.

My goal eventually became sharing with others the insight that was forged in the crucible of real-life personal experience. My heart's great desire is to help people everywhere to cleanse, renew and realign their spirit, mind and body, to find the same balance in every vital area of their life that I did—especially in the areas of family and work—in order to empower them to break through to their full potential.

But there was a price to pay. Just like many other high achievers, I had pushed myself beyond adrenal gland depletion to the point of adrenaline burnout. I had taken great risks, experienced devastating setbacks, gotten my family and life in a big mess, cried out to God and, on the edge of total exhaustion, by grace alone, I received the power to try again. It is sometimes in pain that our greatest contributions are birthed. What you hold in your hands is the fruit of my not giving up. It is now my prayer that it will be a blessing in your life and ideally help you to avoid some of the pains I have known so intimately in my life or help you restore your life with less pain, should you at this time have a need to do so. I pray that you may never cause the pain to your family that I did nor have to go through what I did. Thanks be to God for restoring my life and praise to Him for loving me.

Daily, Scheduled Spiritual Enrichment

> *I know the plans, purpose and destiny I have for you, plans to prosper you and not to harm you, plans to give you hope and a future.* Jeremiah 29:11

Where should we begin but at the beginning of each day? I began to see how important it was to start each morning in a way that sets the proper tone for the entire day. The longer I live, the more I become certain that this is the master key to a fruitful and deeply fulfilling life.

Therefore, the first of the daily, life-building choices is the habit of investing time with God the first thing each morning upon awakening. It sounds extraordinarily simple, but most great truths are simple!

Each one of the truly remarkable people who served as my models for THE DAILY SEVEN makes the choice every day to begin it with the Creator of life. Although they grew up in different cultures and live continents apart, they all agree that there is a God and choose to give gratitude to Him and seek guidance from Him on a daily basis.

How should you go about using the time that you have set aside to spend with God in the morning? Many people have trouble knowing where to begin. Some people decide to read through various Scriptures of the Bible or pray for their needs. As I began the practice of spending morning time with God, I saw the need to use it in seeking first to find out His purpose for my life.

Uncovering Your Purpose

The most important area for which we need God's guidance is understanding His particular purpose for us here on earth. God believes in you and me. We have each been created for a specific purpose, chosen for us by Him. Each of us has been given spiritual gifts to do certain things well, and those gifts make a way for us to fulfill our purpose.

You and I were born for a time such as this and have a specific contribution to make. We all have a spiritual reason for being here. Do you know yours? God wants to share something with the world through you and communicate with them something through your life. You are important because you have something significant to contribute, and there are people in the world who have a need for it. I can assure you that, within your reach right now, there are people who have a need for the gifts you were born to share. As you pour out of your heart what was given to you and use your gifts for the purpose for which they were given with love and in service toward those who have a need for them, you will partake in their abundance and your harvest will be full.

What is it that God wants to give to the world through you? What is it that you can be so great at and bring forth as easily and naturally as a healthy vine produces grapes? Knowing your purpose is of the utmost importance; it is a foundational key to a fruitful and fulfilling life of meaning and significance. So spending time at the beginning of every day with the One who devised the plan for your life makes sense.

What do you love to do so much that you will joyously do it for free? How can you become so outstanding at it that the world's finest organizations and most discerning individuals will long to meet you and offer you top pay to do what you love most? What could you do so well and with so much love that people who experience your excellence want to see you do it again and will bring others to witness the unique expression of your developed gifts?

Often when I ask the above questions, people say they do not know, and they do not know how to find out the answer. The real reason for this lack of knowledge is because the answer is spiritual, and those who are not spiritually connected cannot give a spiritual answer. It is as though they are blind and deaf to God's purposes for them. They are simply not ready to step into and fulfill their unique calling as yet because, without God, there are no real and accurate answers to life's greatest questions.

We are all preprogrammed to yearn for a personal relationship with our Creator. God created us for His pleasure and purposes, and He desires to be in a close, active and daily relationship with us. The key to the revelation (and it is more of a revelation than a discovery) of one's *authentic calling* is in having a personal relationship with God. Finding your calling revealed by Him and faithfully fulfilling it describe the path to the fulfillment you seek.

I believe that you were custom designed specifically for the work God has in mind for you. If you were any different, the people you are meant to reach and help would not be able to relate to you. *You need not be like anyone else to do your part in God's great plan.* They have their niche and you have yours. Focus only on fulfilling your part exceptionally well.

There is a unique greatness in you that is not in me nor is it in anyone else on the face of the earth. But there is one universal feature in everyone's purpose—it will always include service to others. Serving others is the floodgate through which will flow all the potential to do the great works that have been prepared in advance for you by God. You have a unique and special solution for some prevailing problem in this generation. You can help many people. There is something you can do better than most, if not all, people in the world. Find it, develop it and then do it with all your heart with love and in excellence for ever-growing numbers of people. When you find your purpose and follow it, both fulfillment and financial blessings will follow.

My life's purpose, I believe, is to help sincere seekers, especially senior executive leaders in the business world, step out of the maze of confusion and realize their need to be in a personal relationship with God. For me this involves being a catalyst and a guide to help people see their purpose revealed. This is my purpose, what is yours?

I believe the place God brings you to is where there is a deep need for your gift and service; and, as you recognize the need, your heart will long to be of service.

Now, I know from experience this may sound a little too strong for some. I am well aware that many people prefer a non-spiritual, more psychological model, protocol or algorithm for discovering, figuring out, calculating or discerning their purpose or niche.

In my travels across the continents and through the great cities of the earth—from the west to the east, the south to the north—I have very diligently searched for and studied the teachings of many of the most enlightened, famed and respected preachers, gurus and experts. I have personally met many of the greatest authorities and studied the writings of most of the others. After more than a decade I have concluded that the authentic purpose for your life will not be found solely in any particular model, including mine. The real answer will be delivered directly into the heart of each sincere, faith-filled seeker.

Ultimately, finding our purpose is between each of us and God. Authors, teachers and others can be great guides as to how God can use our gifts, but in the end, we need to rely only on God for the revelation of our purpose. We will not find it through focusing just on ourselves in endless introspection, but by focusing on our relationship with God.

Now, with that in mind, I also know that some of these

models provide a useful starting point for many people in their searching and for that reason I offer my humble insights and pray that they may serve you well.

Searching for Your Purpose

How can we begin to search for our purpose? The answer lies within us because God has placed the gifts that we need to fulfill His purpose for our life within us at birth. The following steps are ones that will help you to begin.

1. Prayerfully develop a deep personal relationship with God.

Reflect, contemplate, meditate, pray, and ultimately surrender to Him. Be quiet and still. Listen with your spirit, not with your head. Be sensitive to the quiet voice within and, as valuable insights come to you, journal them.

2. Prayerfully list:
    - Your greatest gifts
    - Your enduring passions
    - Your pain, enduring frustrations, and the greatest struggles you have overcome
    - The deepest needs and greatest wants of other people you are most aware of
    - Your own greatest desires.

    At its roots the word "desire" means "of or from the father," who places good desires in our hearts. He is the one who gave us the gifts that enable us to be of service to others.

As you compile your list, ask God to reveal to you some of the things that have been hidden deep inside you.

3. Prayerfully declare your eagerness, willingness and availability to be used in any way God chooses.

Every day reiterate your acknowledgment of God's love for you and respond with a declaration of your love and trust in Him. As you develop your relationship with Him and declare your willingness to be used by Him, He will gladly share His plans for your life with you.

4. Invest time in solitude, in your "inner room." Study on a mountain, in a desert, near an ocean, in a forest, on the wide-open plains, in a garden, or anyplace where you can be alone, quiet and still. Isolation and solitude is the key.

In the morning make sure the time you have set aside to spend with God is as uninterrupted as it can be. Make your relationship with Him your primary focus. Please understand I am not talking about self-centered introspection, but about a relationship with God, the Creator of life and about your searching for His purposes for your life.

As you daily spend time with God in the morning you can begin to know your purpose in a much clearer way than ever before.

Strategies for Finding Your Purpose

As you develop the list suggested in the previous section and answer the following questions, prayerfully look for natural links, bridges and overlaps among your answers.

☐ What are you naturally good at? What is naturally easy for you to do that other people find intimidating, difficult or unpleasant to do?

☐ How does that connect to, link up with or relate to what you are most passionate about?

☐ What absorbs your attention; what do you love to do with all your heart?

☐ What is it that makes time fly for you?

☐ If you appeared on the *Oprah* show or *Larry King Live* and could share any one message, what would it be? What would you most love to talk about if you could choose the subject? What is your heart full of? What do you talk about the most, and what comes easiest for you to express?

☐ If you could have a national television infomercial, what would you most want to educate people about or promote?

☐ What are your most enduring frustrations? What upsets you the most? What keeps you awake at night?

☐ What is it you feel the strongest about that does not need to be the way it is?

☐ What condition, situation, product or service do you have a better solution for? Why does this frustrate you? Could it be that you are the one gifted and called upon to improve it for many others? Could this be the purpose for which God wants to use you in order to give the solution to those in need?

☐ What pain and challenges have you overcome; can you be a guide for others in these areas?

☐ Where is the greatest or most urgent and growing need you believe you can best fill?

☐ What are your greatest desires, and do many other people share these? Which needs, wants and desires of others are you the most aware of?

☐ Are you both gifted and passionate to provide the solution? Does it frustrate you that people have this want and need? What can you do to fill this need?

☐ How can you be most useful and of the greatest service to others? How can you create and/or add profound value to their lives?

Journal your answers to these questions and keep focusing on serving the needs of others. Dedicate yourself to serving in the best ways you possibly can.

Be patient when working through this fundamental model and invest the necessary time to pray and meditate in solitude for your truest, most authentic answers.

Once you see your vision and hear your calling, *you will never be the same again.* No storm, setback, handicap, rejection, criticism, disappointment, organization, or loss can or will stop you. As you stay close to God, what He begins in you and through you will be completed, even if it takes a lifetime, and it very well may!

Your purpose will not be accomplished by your strength, but by God's power working through you, along with the people He placed in your life for that purpose.

Your purpose may only be revealed to you one doable step at a time; as you faithfully do what must be done, the next step will become clear. Once you see a large portion of your vision, it may both excite and intimidate you due to the size of its scope.

Do not let self-doubt and fear creep in and make you faint of heart, but be of good courage. Let your vision draw you closer to God, just as it is meant to, as you realize that in your own strength, you cannot do it. And when it is done, give credit to God, knowing that you alone could never have accomplished it. The end result will be that the goodness of God will be revealed through you in a unique expression of your God-given gift in service to others. God's words and revelations will never return to Him without accomplishing their purpose.

I encourage you to begin each day prayerfully, giving personal gratitude for your life and all its potential and opportunities. Please do not take all the blessings you have for granted, but see how they fit into His plan for your life. Please do not take your health, family and gifts for granted—they may not always be there. Make the most of them today!

Each day prayerfully give praise to God, seek His guidance and ask boldly for His blessings to help you fulfill His purposes for you.

I encourage you to habitually choose to worship God and pray the first thing each day and the last thing each night, five to 30 minutes or more daily, seven days a week. Do not let the power of prayer stop at the end of its allocated time but let it integrate, gently blend and permeate each moment, choice and action all day long, hard as it may sometimes be.

This daily scheduled time for spiritual enrichment and growth is also a great time for the advanced and mature practitioner for reading, studying and meditating on the Scriptures and appropriate other literature from men and women of God. Be wise and committed enough to get up earlier to extend this special time.

William—A Vision of Possibility

It was just before midnight, as he was lying awake next to his sleeping wife, when William realized that he was on the verge of burnout. He was becoming stale, his health was not taking the strain very well, and he needed to get clarity on the next phase of his life. William wondered what it really was he wanted to do with the rest of his life. He was ready for something new, something more creative and different from his current business career.

The last twenty years had been very busy, and he had enjoyed great success, but now William wanted to create a life where he could experience his dream—to live in a mountain cabin away from the big cities with enough passive and residual income to never again worry about earning a conventional paycheck. Business was good, and their rental-unit real estate portfolio was growing steadily. Their relatively new network marketing downline was also growing exponentially.

The reality, however, was that he did not have quite enough passive income properties or number of distributors in place, as yet, to retire comfortably at the level of security and freedom he dreamed of for his family. Nevertheless he felt overworked and ready for a new path. He was depressed, angry with himself and frustrated. His emotions were telling him to pay attention and to take a new path. He needed new perspective and a new environment. William increasingly felt a need to grow and to contribute in a new way. He was looking for variety in his life, and an assurance of what his niche could be.

William was always an avid reader, but lately he had been so busy that he was too exhausted to enjoy it. He also had a longstanding desire to write a book but was being held back by a certain amount of self-doubt in his ability to write well enough, a seemingly endless lack of enough time, as well as the memory of critical comments from others when he wrote an article some years ago. He remembered that a friend of his recently worked with a great author coach and wondered if that would be a way for him to begin. William realized that deep inside of him was a strong emotional drive to express himself more creatively.

William was always proactive, and he chafed under the constraints of his present life and indecision about his future. Suddenly, surrounded by the silence of the night, he saw the first step he needed to take. He decided to take a vacation in the mountains with his family. His eyes now wide open, he could picture himself relaxing in the solitude of the mountains, investing a little time daily to read again and perhaps to even trying his hand at a little creative writing for an hour or so each day.

It was clear to him that he needed to first invest three or four days relaxing with his family, hiking, soaking in the natural hot springs, watching the sun set, eating three meals a day with them, stargazing, talking and dreaming together. Next he would begin a diligent daily practice of praying about his future and writing the first draft of a manuscript. That plan outlined, William turned over and fell into a peaceful sleep.

A few weeks later, William arrived at the inspiring mountains with his family and began a new regimen that would turn his life around and open up new opportunities for him. He had always been a very self-disciplined person, and right away he began to dedicate an hour early each morning while his family was still asleep to give creative expression to his ideas and the lessons he had learned from life so far. He had a story to tell, one that he believed would touch many people and provide a practical and doable solution to the issues in their lives.

It wasn't easy at first. William had many inner struggles to overcome. Facing a blank page every morning as he sat at his laptop could have been daunting, but he overcame his feelings of inadequacy through prayer. He diligently prayed that his story and insights would be useful and deeply relevant in the lives of millions. As he sought God and began to write his story, he wondered if this was what all his life experiences had prepared him for. He began to see his writing as part of his calling and destiny.

He decided to use his ability and experience in marketing

to make this book a bestseller. His vision was that, God willing, it would be translated into a multitude of languages and reach people everywhere, making a real difference in their lives and helping them to make their world a better place for all. William longed to help people experience more love, passion and gratitude, a deeper sense of meaning and purpose, and ultimately, a more abundant life filled with peace and joy.

William's vision was an honorable one, and his gifts facilitated its implementation. After its publication, his book was sold all across the country and in London, Japan, Singapore, Taiwan, Korea, Australia, Nigeria, China, Brazil and beyond. Writing was certainly not always an easy path for him to follow, but then, nothing worth doing ever is. Against all odds he became a best-selling, published author with the help of his family, friends, author coach and publisher, and everyone involved benefited tremendously.

Sales on the internet began to boom after his friend Wade helped him design a highly effective dynamic site that inspired and educated the visitors. Total book sales now counted in the millions. Men and women everywhere were encouraged to commit themselves to a higher standard of godly success and become people of influence, impact and significance.

William sold most of his business shares and became truly free, traveling as a popular speaker, television and radio talk show guest, and retreat workshop leader. Quite often he traveled with his family from their new log home in the mountains of Colorado. They divided their time according to the seasons between their dream log cabin in a small town about ninety minutes from Denver International in

Colorado and their second home in Hawaii. There he loved to reflect with a heart full of gratitude on their large veranda. In Colorado he enjoyed doing simple things such as chopping firewood, cooking a great soup and taking in the silence and vistas as he drove down to a nearby town in their old red truck for supplies. He still enjoyed signing books at bookstores, giving talks, meeting new people and reaching millions of people via the many talk shows, but there remained a lot to be said for a slower-paced and more simple life of greater balance—exactly what his book encouraged others to work towards. He was living his dream, at peace and deeply fulfilled. This was indeed the stuff dreams are made of. But how did he get so lucky you might ask?

The only way he could possibly answer that question was that luck is nothing short of God's favor in people's lives. He knew that his success was by God's favor, for he had prayed sincerely in faith that God would use him for His purposes. He always remembered the verses that said to seek the rightousnesss of God first and his heart's desires would be added to him. He felt strongly that if he worked diligently to fulfill God's purposes for his life, he too could live his dream. He also knew that if it had not been for the many people God brought into his life to help him along the way, he could not possibly have succeeded with the book at the level he had. He had experienced God's favor and was humbly grateful for it.

Questions to Contemplate

☐ What do you want to do with the rest of your life? What might be the highest use of your time and talents? What will fulfill you most? What is it that your heart longs and yearns for? What could be your greatest contribution be and what could be the catalyst needed for you to accomplish it?

☐ What do you need to read, and what could you write that could be profoundly valuable in the lives of others?

☐ How can you best create a life of true, abundant prosperity and deep love and meaning for your family, others and yourself?

☐ What would satisfy your deepest needs? What would give you more significance, love, connection with others, and gratitude? What could be your inspiration and generational legacy?

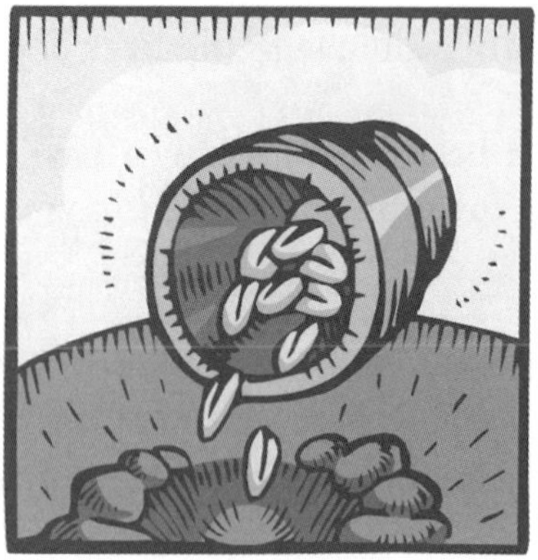

Chapter 2

The Developed Mind

Daily, Scheduled Mental Development

Practice number two—daily scheduled mental development—follows naturally after reading, studying, memorizing and or contemplating sacred Scripture. This mental activity includes absorbing high value secular information and knowledge that will make you more useful because of the increase in your ability to contribute more effectively. Invest time in gaining cutting-edge, in-demand, and profound, timeless knowledge and wisdom.

In your journal, note the answers to the following questions:

☐ What expertise is experiencing a growing demand in the global marketplace?

☐ What can you study and learn at a deeper level than most people care to do, which will enable you to solve a problem that increasing numbers of people—or even multinational corporations—have an increasing need for?

☐ What can you read, study and learn that will inspire you, challenge you, and make you a more sought after person today, tomorrow and beyond? What will be in demand in the future? Does it align well with your niche?

Once you focus on a specific area of knowledge, first read all the greatest classics ever written on that subject, and then study at least the ten latest, most authoritative and popular works on the subject. Summarize all the principles and best thinking in a journal specifically for this subject in order to create your own database of insights.

By the time you have read, studied and summarized every significant work ever published on your chosen subject, you will have become an extremely knowledgeable person. With enough practical experience to add to it, you can become a leading authority.

I strongly believe that new knowledge, at the right time in your life, can change your life forever if you will let it. One paragraph, one statement, one question, or one meeting with someone very special could be the catalyst that opens the doorway to a new aspect of life, or be the final piece of your personal puzzle that makes everything click into place for you.

Do yourself a favor and do the following three things:

1. Obtain a library card and become a daily student of the greatest classics of all time.

All the greatest people who ever lived are waiting at the library to teach you the collective wisdom of time gone by. Read biographies and autobiographies; study books on spirituality, family, relationships, philosophy, leadership, communication, sales, investing, health, law, management and more. First cover a broad base, then focus intensely on one high value, useful, and in-demand focus area and its supporting domains.

2. Build up a personal library of great books.

Great books are resources you can turn to again and again for their wisdom and insight.

3. Keep detailed learning journals. Record the best of all you learn from many sources and let it become part of how you choose to live and serve as a foundation for your own thinking.

A LITTLE STORY FROM AFRICA

In Africa, the story is told of an American missionary who was distributing Bibles in a village. When he offered a copy to one of the men in the village the man is reported to have said, "If I take your book I am going to use the pages to roll my tobacco in and smoke it." The missionary replied that it would be fine providing the man promised to read each page first before he smoked it. He also stipulated that the man should start reading the four gospels.

Some years later the missionary was both surprised and delighted to see the very same man at a conference as a speaker and to hear how he smoked Matthew, Mark and Luke, and how when he read John, Acts, and Romans he could not smoke it anymore! Reading a little each day, he became transformed. The Bible changed his life, and it was evident since he had become an active itinerant messenger and teacher of the Word.

What message could change your life so dramatically? Somewhere there is a book, quote or poem that is waiting for you that will speak very directly and personally to you and make all the difference. Go find it. Perhaps within you there is a set of words someone else needs that you must write and publish. I encourage you to do it.

I encourage you to invest some time in the great libraries of the world and in bookstores big and small. You never know what or where your trigger will be found. Become a great student. The old saying, "Readers are leaders," is a true one.

☐ During your daily time allocation for mental development, read at least one great, inspirational, motivational and/or educational how-to paragraph or page. Reflect on it and journal it. Learn some new words, since they are the software of our thinking, and as you expand your vocabulary you expand your capacity to think and to express yourself with greater clarity.

☐ Do some creative journaling. Plan, set goals, visualize, contemplate and write creatively.

☐ Write some leadership, sales or investment questions and impact statements as scripts, and rehearse and integrate them into your heart, speech and actions.

☐ Think how you can ask better questions, and understand what questions you should be asking. You can begin by asking questions such as "What if it were possible to...." and "How can...."

☐ Ask, what is new, what is next, and how can I either be first with it or leverage it?

☐ Ask, how can I give more for less, combine, reduce, increase, and improve...?

☐ Schedule at least 15 minutes or more each morning for your mental development and build ever-increasing knowledge and skills that are in demand. You will be glad you did. You will be surprised how quickly 15 to 30 minutes adds up and improves your capacity to be, do, give, and have more.

Chapter 3

The Physically Conditioned Body

Daily, Scheduled Physical Conditioning

The third of THE DAILY SEVEN scheduled lifestyle choices and action habits—physical conditioning—is a very commonly neglected habit.

In the United States, increasing numbers of people lie to themselves by thinking and saying they do not have enough time for a little regular exercise until their physician one day gives them some news that shocks them into action. You do not need to be one of them, but if you already are, you will find this section immensely valuable.

When people say they do not have time to take care of their health, it is a sure sign that they are out of control. It tells you volumes about their values and is proof that their life is out of balance.

Diet alone is not the best long-term strategy to be properly conditioned physically. We all need to find sustainable ways to make exercise our primary strategy for good health, body-fat loss, improved production and performance capacity, enhanced appearance, and increased energy.

Again, how and where do we begin? The following is one good way to create a healthy active lifestyle that will provide you with the energy you need to fulfill your purpose in life.

Your New Body System

1. Exercise with dumbbells, medicine balls, or kettlebells three times per week—on Mondays, Wednesdays and Fridays—early in the morning, before breakfast for up to 30 minutes.

2. Energy walk, "breathe" walk and reflective walk on Tuesdays, Thursdays and Saturday mornings before breakfast for up to 30 minutes. Utilize a pedometer and walk from 4,000 to 12,000 steps per day, including all your normal daily walking. The secret is to increase your movement. SIT LESS, MOVE MORE.

SAMPLE 8-WEEK EXERCISE SCHEDULE

Monday - Dumbbell Workout I
Tuesday - Energy Walk

Wednesday - Dumbbell Workout II
Thursday - Energy & "Breathe" Walk
Friday - Dumbbell Workout III
Saturday - Reflective Walk
Sunday - Gentle Resting & Stretching

> WARNING: THIS PROGRAM MAY NOT BE SUITABLE FOR EVERYONE AND IS ONLY INTENDED FOR HEALTHY ADULTS WITH THE EXPLICIT APPROVAL OF THEIR OWN PHYSICIAN.

You may want to substitute some activities with ones more suitable for your own individual preferences. Other ideas include Pilates, cycling, mountain biking, running, swimming or rowing. Having said that, know that those who include resistance training with weights in their program can expect the best results.

Regardless of your choices, we highly recommend you perform the exercise in the following ways:

1. Exercise on a regular schedule, gradually increasing the resistance.

2. Exercise on an empty stomach (other than water, green tea or whey protein).

3. Exercise before breakfast, early in the morning, six days per week, 50 weeks per year.

Exercise performed before breakfast may be more effective in kick-starting and elevating one's metabolism, and it enables one to burn more fat more effectively.

4. Adapt your program every eight weeks to ensure continued effectiveness and to break the monotony. To burn more fat you need more muscle, and to build more muscle you need increased weight loads and demand.

5. If you choose to stick to this program for a second phase, at a minimum increase the weight of the dumbbells and walk faster and further in the same amount of time.

6. Add new exercises from time to time to ensure balance and variety.

I encourage you to invest in a pedometer, log book/journal, body fat % scale, cross-trainer shoes, walking socks, 3 to 5 sets of dumbbells, medicine balls, or kettlebells of increasing weight, a basic adjustable weight training bench or large exercise ball, a blender, a portable disk player and inspirational music.

MONDAYS

DUMBBELL WORKOUT 1

First, stretch to warm up adequately, and take at least seven deep, energizing breaths. Breathe slowly; exhale twice as slowly as you inhale.

TOUCH THE EARTH; TOUCH THE SKY

Your health permitting, begin with a light dumbbell, kettlebell, or medicine ball and increase the demand by gradually building up to increasingly heavier resistance.

Place a single dumbbell vertically between your feet. Standing, drop deep in your knees with your back straight; with both hands on the dumbbell, begin a smooth pull upwards with your legs as you begin to inhale deeply.

Next, let your forearms, biceps, abdominals, lower and upper back muscles and shoulder muscles continue the pull until the dumbbell is high above your head, as you breathe out. Return the dumbbell to its starting position. Lower it in a smooth and controlled manner along the same muscle pathway.

This is an absolutely fantastic metabolic activator that conditions about 90% or more of all your muscles, even your calves, either directly or indirectly as stabilizing muscles. The only muscle groups that may need some additional work are your chest and triceps. This is easily done with dumbbell bench presses and/or press-ups. Perform up to five sets of 21, 18, 12, 8, and 6 repetitions with increasingly heavier weights for each set. These large movement resistance exercises are very effective. In as little as 4 to 12 minute sessions of regularly doing this exercise, you will see fantastic results.

Note: ever increasing demand on your system is essential to continually stimulate new muscle growth. Since this exercise program is primarily structured for health and fitness, it is predominantly the last three sets of repetitions that will build new muscle, provided adequately heavy weights are used. Remember, muscle is what facilitates fat burn. Muscle is the furnace that burns body fat. Build some muscle—every ounce helps.

These dumbbell exercises will not result in excessive muscle development. What this program can do is to build a healthier and leaner body that will increase your overall sense of well being, self-esteem, confidence, performance and appearance—all for an investment of less than 30 minutes, 3 times per week. I believe this investment of time is one of the best you can make.

On days when you are under severe time pressure, just perform one set of 21 repetitions. It will take you two minutes or less and give you a great metabolic boost, as well as keep you in the habit of doing this fantastic, total body-shaping drill.

DUMBBELL BENCH PRESS

Three sets of 12, 8 and 6 repetitions or five sets of maximum repetition press ups.

You can alternate 45-degree angle incline dumbbell workouts with flat dumbbell bench presses for each workout if you choose to do so.

WEDNESDAYS

DUMBBELL WORKOUT 2

Warm up with gentle stretching, and take seven long, deep, slow breaths.

DUMBBELL POWER BUILDERS

Your health permitting, begin with a light dumbbell or kettlebell placed between your feet. Standing over it, place one hand palm facing out behind your lower back and squat deep and wide in your knees* with your back straight, buttocks low and head up. Lift the dumbbell up and overhead in one smooth long movement as you inhale. Keep your elbows slightly bent; let your legs, buttocks, abdominals and back muscles do most of the work.

The aim is always to activate and stimulate as many of the largest muscles as possible. As you become more conditioned, you may hold a second and eventually heavier weight stationary behind your back for extra resistance. Perform up to five sets of 21, 18, 12, 8 and 6 repetitions. This is a great exercise for toning your buttocks, quadriceps, hamstrings, abdominals, lower back and shoulders.

**Deep squats are not recommended for people with knee joint problems.*

DUMBBELL ONE-ARM, BENT OVER ROW

Three sets of 21, 18 and 12 repetitions for females; three sets of 12, 8 and 6 repetitions, with heavier weights, for males.

FRIDAYS

DUMBBELL WORKOUT 3

Warm up with gentle stretching and take seven long, slow, deep breaths.

DUMBBELL FAT AND MUSCLE BLASTER

Your health permitting, begin with two dumbbells or kettlebells, one each placed alongside each foot. Use a slightly narrow stance. Keep your back straight and your head up. Pull up using your legs as you begin to inhale forcefully. As you reach the standing position, curl the dumbbells/kettlebells up to your shoulders and dynamically complete the movement by performing an overhead shoulder press as you exhale. Upon return, again keep your back straight; let your legs, buttocks and abdominals do much of the work.

This is a very demanding exercise and, therefore, a fantastic metabolic booster, muscle builder and shaper, and fat burner. Perform up to five sets of 21, 18, 12, 8 and 6 repetitions.

DOUBLE SIT UP/BENCH KNEE UPS

Lie flat on your back with your arms together, stretched out above your head with your feet together. As you exhale, curl up to your midsection catching your knees at the center.

At a much more advanced level, you can pass an increasingly heavier ball between your hands and feet for greater muscle stimulation and results.

For unconditioned people we recommend you begin with the following fantastic exercise: Sit sideways at the center of a sturdy exercise bench, with your feet together. Lift your knees towards your chest and push your feet back in a controlled manner, without touching the floor. Inhale as you pull your knees up.

Perform up to five sets of 12 repetitions of one or both of these abdominal drills. As you become more conditioned, you may choose to use increasingly heavier balls between your feet with the bench knee up, with a set and repetition protocol of five sets of 21, 18, 12, 8 and 6 repetitions. The choice is yours.

Note: we recommend you follow this 3-part new body plan for a minimum of 8 weeks and up to 12 or 16 weeks and then consult with a suitably qualified and experienced trainer to create a more personalized program specific to your own needs.

Should you, for medical reasons, not be able to perform this routine at all, we suggest you consult with a team consisting of your own physician, chiropractor and trainer, to develop a program suitable for you.

TUESDAYS, THURSDAYS, AND SATURDAYS

ENERGY WALK

Energy walking simply means walking at a fast pace, breathing deeply and rhythmically, and with a dynamic posture, including large arm movements.

Your health permitting, start out gently, and as you become more conditioned and as the body warms up, begin to walk more energetically, faster, and more dynamically. Let your intuition guide you; do not overdo it.

We recommend you use a heart rate monitor and only perform energy walking with a physician's approval. Stay within your ideal safe heart rate zone as discussed with your physician. If during the exercise you cannot talk with relative comfort, you may be overdoing it and be at risk.

You may consider employing a very light set of mini dumbbells, specially designed for power walking, and listen to inspirational, motivational or educational recordings while you walk.

Recruit a walk buddy and use a pedometer to count your steps. A logbook is absolutely essential.

Walk early in the morning, before breakfast. Ideally enjoy another gentler walk every night within minutes after dinner, if at all possible, even if it is walking in place in your home. There are fantastic specially weighted shoes available as an option for those who want to work more exercise into their daily activity.

We recommend you wear your pedometer all day long, every day, and aim to walk an average of 8000 or more steps total per day, including your exercise walks and normal daily movement. The essential key is to increase your overall daily movement.

"BREATHE" WALK

"Breathe" walking is a slightly more gentle form of walking than the super intense energy walk and involves a much higher awareness and focus on deep rhythmical breathing. A popular way is to inhale for 2 to 5 consecutive steps i.e., inhale, inhale, inhale through your nose with your mouth closed and exhale, exhale, exhale as sharp exhalations through your mouth.

REFLECTIVE WALK

Reflective walking is a very quiet, slow, gentle and relaxing walk with a higher awareness of one's surroundings and emotions; therefore, it is best done in a safe, tranquil place of great natural beauty such as an ocean, lake, forest, park or garden. With great focus on slow, full and gentle breathing, it is meant to be a more spiritual experience and may include prayer, praise and worship from a grateful heart.

Note: the after dinner walk is ideally a family affair with much greater benefits than just aiding digestion.

A FAT-LOSS PLAN THAT WORKS

YOUR ACTION PLAN:

STEP 1 - GET REAL

Stand lightly clothed in front of a full-length mirror in good light, take a long, hard look, and be honest with yourself. How does what you see make you feel? Have you been guilty of neglect?

STEP 2 - SET A GOAL

Set a personal goal to achieve a realistic and healthy fat-loss goal, measured in % body fat, by a specific celebration date. Have your body fat % measured to have a basis for your goal setting and have a compelling enough personal reason to follow through.

STEP 3 - KEEP GOOD RECORDS

Have a high quality "before" photograph taken, preferably in a bathing suit, and stick it on your refrigerator door.

Post your personal fat-loss goal card and an inspirational picture of someone who has a similar baseline body type as you, who is in a similar age group and was as overweight as you, and who lost it all to look as good as they do.

Also post your % body fat on the refrigerator door and update your status every 14 days.

Keep a graph showing body fat % decrease and lean muscle mass increase. Forget actual body weight as a sound measurement. It does not reflect muscle-to-body fat ratio and composition, which is what really matters.

Muscle weighs more than fat, so you may begin to weigh a little more due to increased muscle growth and density at first; yet, you will look much slimmer and toned in your buttocks, abdominals and thighs, and enjoy good definition in your shoulders, back and arms. You will feel like a million!

STEP 4 - RECRUIT A PARTNER

Ideally your spouse should go on this action plan with you for optimum results. Keep each other motivated and hold each other accountable.

STEP 5 - GET YOUR PHYSICIAN'S APPROVAL AND ADVICE

Be open about your intentions and goal. Get a comprehensive physical examination relating to your intention and ask your physician for specific recommendations.

STEP 6 - GO SHOPPING

Clear your refrigerator and pantry of all the foods that are not on our recommended food list and fill them with what is on the list. (See the next chapter for details.)

Very important—keep a food journal of everything you eat and drink. Record what you consume, the time, quantity and how it was prepared (boiled, grilled, microwaved, etc.).

Equip yourself with dumbbells, medicine balls, and/or kettlebells, an exercise mat, a large exercise ball, adjustable weight bench, cross trainer shoes, walking socks, a pedometer, heart rate monitor, log book/ journal, blender, active sitting disk, etc.

STEP 7 - GO FOR IT

Now, no more excuses! Begin your new body system no later than tomorrow morning. Work those dumbbells and walk those steps with no compromise, no excuses. Log each daily workout in detail.

Follow your exercise plan consistently for an absolute minimum of 8 to 16 weeks and then judge the results by how you look and feel, not by how much you weigh.

Remain accountable for at least eight weeks. Do not miss a single workout, as each workout counts. If you do miss a workout, let it only be one and get back on track immediately. If this happens in the first eight weeks, restart the eight-week challenge all over again.

John and Cathy—New Beginnings

John is a big man in his forties, a discerning man with very high personal standards and solid values, a really loving, caring man with deep faith, a high work ethic and prosperous business. He is truly one of the kindest, most generous and fun people you will ever meet, and a great chef and photographer as well. In spite of all that, John began to feel a little depressed and very frustrated as he struggled with his weight and, as a result, also his health in general.

Cathy, born in the midwest, and more recently living in northern California, is a widowed single mom with two young kids. She is a former model, still very attractive and energetic. Her friends all say that she is a positive, caring person and above all, a God-loving woman. Sophisticated, elegant, soft spoken, feminine, financially responsible, a little vivacious, and full of chutzpa, she is a little bit overweight and out of shape after a few struggling years. Cathy was now fast becoming a successful distributor. She is both a popular and ambitious group leader for a large network marketing company, her downline one of the fastest growing in the region.

She is exactly the kind of woman John had dreamed about all his life. They had instant rapport the moment they met; they loved the same kind of music and shared the same standards, values and dreams for the future. John was now rather overweight after the last few stressful and busy years had taken their toll, and the physical neglect was now catching up. Cathy too was beginning to notice her body was not what it used to be, and that "something had to be done." In fact those were the exact words John's physician used. John and Cathy both loved great food and traveled to distant places where they typically overate. And with their busy lifestyles, they had both fallen out of the habit of regular exercise.

John and Cathy were planning to get married and honeymoon in beautiful Cape Town, South Africa, where they were going to stay in a castle, high in the mountains above Hout Bay. It would be summer there, and they both made a commitment to each other to get into the best shape possible beforehand. They agreed to hold each other accountable and do at least two workouts per week together.

John's heart was in his decision but a shoulder and lower back injury at first held him back. He determined to find a way to get in shape, so he began to stretch and walk daily. He certainly could not run at first and soon realized he did not need to. His initial progress was frustratingly slow, but he persevered and began walking more than 10,000 steps a day. He started to see real results, and this progress was deeply satisfying and motivating. John wore special weighted walking shoes and a pedometer everyday and was amazed at how it was paying off. He got in the habit of parking further away in parking lots to facilitate more walking. He even kept a detailed, daily walking log book. Although the first week he felt more tired than usual, the next week he was delighted with newfound levels of energy, and he looked and felt younger. He slept better and his mind was so much clearer. He decided that although he should have started on this plan years ago, he was sure glad he was doing it now. He swam two days a week with Cathy, which did wonders for his muscle tone and the rehabilitation of his shoulder.

Cathy was fortunate not to have old nagging injuries and started to swim daily right away, and began weight resistance training at home with just a medicine ball, five sets of dumbbells, a Swiss ball, exercise mat and bench. She typically alternated a day of intense swimming and brief, yet intense, weight workout three days per week, with light swimming and a long, rather fast walk on the days in between. She loved the result. Everyone noticed not just the amazing transformation of her body, but also the positive renewal of her mind and spirit. She became a true inspiration to everyone who met and knew her. It was certainly not easy for her to make time every morning to work out, especially with two kids to get to school, but she did it and was glad she did. With a conventional job she certainly would have found it much more difficult, although doable, but she was thankful that with her successful and growing network marketing business she had a bit more freedom. Cathy even found time for two Pilates classes per week. She loved being active again. They both would look great in their wedding photographs.

One evening on a romantic dinner date, John could not stop looking with admiration at Cathy. They discussed how absolutely worthwhile all their efforts had been and how sad they would have looked and felt just five years in the future had they not made this commitment to each other.

Questions to Contemplate

☐ Are you in as great a shape as you could be and want to be?

☐ What could inspire and compel you into taking better care of your physical body, now?

☐ Who could be your workout and/or accountability partner? How could you best coordinate your day planners to workout at least two or three times per week and enjoy the process?

☐ What would your percentage of body fat be when you are in great shape?

☐ How can you best achieve your goals in a healthful way, and how great will that make you feel?

☐ What do you need to start doing now and why?

☐ When will you be in awesome shape, how will that specifically look, and what is your personal celebration date?

Chapter 4

Intelligent Nutrition

Daily, Scheduled Portion-Controlled Nutrition

In the United States today, increasing numbers of people are overfed, undernourished, out of shape, overweight or even morbidly or clinically obese, and suffering from a number of debilitating diseases.

The fourth daily choice and action habit is that of daily, scheduled portion-controlled nutrition. This involves enjoying four to seven small, nutrient-dense meals a day, at regularly scheduled times.

In addition to the nutritious meals, also ensure an adequate intake of micro-nutrients (vitamins and minerals) with one or more high quality supplements, including a multi-vitamin, ideally in liquid form for faster and greater absorption. During times of increased workout stress and especially when peak performance is required, you may want to supplement with key nutrients such as the following amino acids and micronutrients: Alanine, Arginine, Leucine, Isoleucine, Taurine, Valine, Creatine, and Glutamine as well as antioxidants, especially vitamins C and E. Also ensure a good supply of vitamin B-complex with fresh whole foods daily.

RECOMMENDED LONG-TERM MACRO-NUTRIENT RATIOS

- 49% low and medium glycemic index carbohydrates
- 31% proteins of high quality
- 20% good fats

This is the recommended optimum macro-nutrient ratio mix, measured as a % of total calories consumed.

The 49-31-20% ratio is ideal for healthy, hard-working, actively exercising, fun-loving individuals with high-energy requirements and who are committed to feeling and looking the best they possibly can.

For fat loss, some people may need to reduce their carbohydrate intake to about 39% and increase their protein intake up to 41%. Nutrition requirements vary for individuals; however, most active people may benefit from enjoying at least one gram of protein and two grams of complex carbohydrates per pound of bodyweight and a minimum of one gram of essential fatty acids per day.

Eat a colorful and large variety of foods in moderate portion sizes from mixed sources at regular times each day.

A word on fats: enjoy mostly monounsaturated and polyunsaturated fats, with less saturated fat, and avoid trans fats. Let your fats predominantly come from fish, avocados, walnuts, almonds, flax oil and olive oil. Aim for a ratio of 8% or more polyunsaturated fats (fish, walnuts, pumpkin seeds, borage oil); 7% monosaturated fats (avocado, almonds, olives, olive oil) and 5% or less saturated fats (milk, meat, cheese). Remember, your body needs adequate dietary fat to enable you to burn body fat most effectively and to enable certain key organic functions.

RECOMMENDED CORE FOOD LIST

PROTEINS
Eggs (Whites)
Salmon (Alaskan sockeye)
Tuna (Albacore/Yellowfin)
Flounder
Haddock
Halibut
Cod
Grouper
Red Snapper
Orange Roughy
Sardines

Bass
Haddock
Herring
Mackerel
Mahi-Mahi
Mullet
Rock Fish
Tilapia
Pollock
Whiting
Trout
Sole
Whey
Skinless chicken breasts
Skinless turkey breasts
Non-fat cottage cheese
Non-fat plain yogurt
Skimmed milk

CARBOHYDRATES

FRUITS

Apples
Peaches
Pears
Plums
Oranges
Tangerines
Kiwi
Grapefruit
Papaya
Mangoes

Cantaloupe
Honeydew melon
Cherries
Strawberries
Pineapples
Blackberries
Figs
Blueberries
Grapes
Raspberries
Bananas
Prunes
Raisins
Dried apricots
Star fruit

VEGETABLES
Asparagus
Artichokes
Alfalfa sprouts
Barley
Beets
Broccoli
Brussel sprouts
Beans (pinto, black, kidney, lima, navy)
Bean sprouts
Cauliflower
Cabbage
Celery
Cucumber
Chickpeas
Carrots
Collards
Corn

Edamame
Eggplant
Green beans
Kale
Lentils
Lettuce
Onion
Parsnips
Peppers
Potatoes
Pumpkin
Radish
Spinach
Squash
Sweet potatoes
Tomatoes
Watercress
Zucchini

FATS
Almonds
Avocado
Borage oil
Brazil nuts
Cashew nuts
Evening Primrose oil
Flax oil
Hazel nuts
Macadamia nuts
Olive oil
Olives
Wheat germ oil
Walnuts

OTHER PRODUCTS
Lemons
Wheat grass
Sea vegetables such as kelp and other "super green foods," especially green barley grass
All natural peanut butter and or almond butter
Herbs and spices, including cinnamon and paprika.
Green and black tea
Fat-free and soymilk
Sunflower, flax and pumpkin seeds
Rye and/or whole wheat bread
Honey
Tofu
Olives

Note: be sure to drink at least eight large servings of water daily. Understand that it is fine to occasionally enjoy a small portion of beef filet, liver, sirloin or lean ground beef if you so choose.

SAMPLE ONE DAY MEAL PLAN

PRE-WORKOUT

Two glasses of water or one cup of green tea. Or an 8 oz. whey protein shake and another 8 oz. or more immediately post-workout.

POST-WORKOUT BREAKFAST (IDEALLY WITHIN 30 MINUTES AFTER YOUR WORKOUT).

- 1 Grapefruit

- 2 to 4 hard-boiled egg whites
- 1 medium bowl of slow-cooked oatmeal with 10 raisins and 10 almonds or walnuts and a little cinnamon;
  or a large bowl of mixed fruit salad with two desert spoons of fat-free yogurt, 5 walnuts and 5 almonds;
  or a power smoothie with whey, green barley grass, water or skimmed milk, fruits—one banana/half a cup of berries and 10 almonds or walnuts.
- 1 glass of water and supplements

10:00 AM MID-MORNING SNACK

8 to 16 oz. high-quality protein shake with water, soy or fat free milk with 1 piece of fruit or a protein-rich whole food based meal replacement bar.

12:3O LUNCH

One rye/whole-wheat bread sandwich with 5 oz tuna/salmon/sirloin steak/2 boiled egg whites/grilled skinless chicken breasts and a small mixed green salad with lettuce, tomatoes, cucumber, carrots, green and black olives, fresh lemon juice and flax oil or extra-virgin olive oil.

3:00 PM MID-AFTERNOON SNACK

One high-quality protein bar or a handful of unsalted nuts and raisins, and/or an apple and a glass of water.

7:00 PM DINNER

One 4 oz. to 6 oz. grilled fish/grilled skinless chicken breast, with two or three low glycemic load vegetables of choice from the recommended core food list. Great choices include baked sweet potato, steamed brown rice, broccoli or spinach. Remember: include colorful veggies and ensure variety.

9:00 PM NUTRITIOUS SNACK

8 oz L-glutamine rich whey protein shake with 50% soy or skimmed milk and 50% water, or two large tablespoons of non-fat cottage cheese and 8 fl oz skimmed milk or water.

Note: enjoy carbohydrates along with proteins and good essential fats with all three of your core meals. Allow yourself more generous helpings of carbohydrates and essential fats with your post-workout breakfast, the single most important meal of the day.

I also encourage you to enjoy more green leaf vegetables with either lunch or dinner or both, and super green foods such as sea vegetables, green barley grass, wheat grass, and spurilina supplements.

With most meals, especially your core main meals, balance your protein and carbohydrate intake to approximately equal amounts measured in volume. One popular and common measurement method is to use the size of one's own palm or fist; or, to be precise, measure by weight.

There is no need to make your nutritional plan any more complicated than this. Keep it simple and sustainable.

Michelle—From Fat to Fabulous

Michelle, already into a fairly regular exercise routine, just celebrated her birthday and was not happy with her body at all. She felt fat, and admittedly her habitual dietary patterns were out of control. She recently read a survey that stated that the average American consumer diet consists of up to 80% carbohydrates and more, mostly in bad carbs, and realized she probably fell into that category.

She knew that something had to change, but she wasn't sure if she could really cut back on the pasta, pizzas and cake she so loved, not to mention the chocolate and ice cream.

Michelle was rather fashion conscious and loved to dress well, but lately she was forced to buy a dress one size larger than before, and that really bothered her, especially after realizing even it was a little too tight on her. She had been in an emotional mess lately—having problems both in her career and personal life the last couple of months—that she had not taken adequate care of herself.

Michelle knew that it's smart to make exercise one's primary strategy for losing weight, and that improved muscle tone facilitates more effective fat metabolism, but she also needed to become more knowledgeable and intelligent about her nutrition. Her personal trainer, a former boyfriend, always used to say she had an awesome base structure, and that if she just trained a little harder and ate a lot better, she would have one of the best head-turning figures in town. She decided that she had enough of feeling fat; she committed herself to eating well.

In fact she decided to stop meeting with her two current friends and reach out to make new friends with healthier habits. She saw that a new girl at work seemed to be a very refined person, spirituality discerning, with good habits of eating and working out and decided to spend time with her.

She also decided to ask her older sister, Pam, who just recently had a baby and who had gotten back into beautiful shape very quickly, to advise her. She always admired her and her husband for being such smart, disciplined and healthy eaters, consistently in great shape and full of energy.

Pam agreed that to make this work long term Michelle was going to need a new peer group, one with sounder habits. Pam explained how smart nutrition affects up to 70% of the look great/feel fabulous equation. She told her that it really is a combination of eating the right kinds of foods in smaller portions with the right ratio of good quality proteins, complex low glycemic load carbohydrates, and some essential fats. She talked with Michelle about super greens such as fresh, young, green barley grass, wheatgrass and spirulina, and the vital importance of adequate hydration with purified water for one's health, skin beauty and energy levels.

Michelle's sister recommended that she eat more fresh fruits and vegetables, complex carbohydrates, and healthy fats. She recommended more water rich foods and healthier proteins. She emphasized colorful foods in as great a variety as possible. For cravings she recommended first a glass of water, and in extreme emergencies, an apple with just a very light sprinkle of salt to boost both one's blood sugar and blood pressure a little. She even recommended extra dark organic chocolate as an occasional treat, but not in the evening.

To Michelle's surprise, her sister also suggested that she eat more frequently in smaller amounts; stop drinking sodas; and take high quality supplements, at least a multivitamin rich in antioxidants, especially vitamins C and E with breakfast. She also told Michelle to get more sleep, since lack of sleep releases more stress hormones, increases sugar cravings and adds more belly fat.

Michelle's sister took a "before" photograph of her and told her to stick it on her refrigerator door, with a promise to contrast it with a really awesome "after" picture in 8 to 12 weeks. That was to be Michelle's challenge. She called her sister daily for an accountability chat, to ensure she stayed on track, and they met in person once a week for a body-fat percentage assessment, and body weight check once every 14 days. Looking at her before photograph, Michelle also realized how poor her posture was. She recalled that her sister, who is also a personal growth life coach, explained how we can change how we feel by just improving our posture. As soon as Michelle decided to walk tall again, the change in how she felt was almost instantaneous.

By the fourth week Michelle really got into it, and by the end of week six she could not believe how much better she felt and looked. She just loved all the compliments and attention she was now getting. It seemed like all of a sudden everybody wanted to be friends with her, and by week 12 she had become a magnet for men at work.

The combination of intelligent eating, brief yet intense daily workouts, alternating resistance training with moderately heavy dumbbells, cardio training with lots of walking and swimming, getting enough quality sleep, hydrating with purified water, and stretching daily was really paying off. She loved how much easier she moved since she started stretching daily. She decided that she could never go back to her old lifestyle again. She vividly saw what a difference just twelve committed weeks could make. She loved her new lifestyle and enjoyed preparing wonderful, healthy meals for her many new friends.

Michelle had now become a new person, so much more confident, positive, and fun to be with. If asked for her best advice, she would say, "Go for it girls, you will look and feel much more gorgeous than you do right now. If I can change, anyone can."

Here is a sample daily meal plan she recommends:

Start with purified water upon waking, and continue to drink small sips every ten to fifteen minutes during your workout. Drink a carbohydrate and whey protein rich meal replacement drink within 15 to 30 minutes after your workout. Michelle's favorite post-workout smoothie is 50% purified water, 50% soy or skimmed milk, an entire packet of blueberries, 7 almonds, five walnuts and a teaspoon of ground flax seeds, with 20-40 grams of whey protein, and some green barley grass blended and liquefied with a little ice. She just loves its color, taste and energizing power. She also loves it with a banana for variety.

After an all-out, weight-training session, or intense swimming session, she also loves a grapefruit, two boiled egg whites, and a slice of whole wheat toast as an alternative breakfast or even in addition to her smoothie.

Mid-morning, as well as mid-afternoon she enjoys an apple and an organic whole food bar, additional protein shake, or a fresh shot of wheatgrass.

For lunch, Michelle recommends a whole wheat sandwich with chopped boiled egg whites, or turkey or chicken breast, baby spinach leaves, crumbled walnuts with just a little organic fig jam to bind it together or fat-free cottage cheese. It is inexpensive, fast to make, easy to transport, healthy and delicious.

Dinner is her most favorite meal—grilled fish, especially Alaskan wild salmon, or chicken breast, a brown and wild rice mix, a small lettuce salad with red, green, orange or yellow sweet bell peppers and tomato, with a few drops of olive oil and a little bit of lemon juice. On days she trains really hard, she also eats two or three spoons of fat-free cottage cheese for its l-glutamine for muscle recovery at about 9 pm.

She drinks water with all her meals and between, and to reduce the risk of craving and eating something sweet after dinner, she drinks some purified water and brushes her teeth immediately afterwards. Since she started to nourish her body more completely, she noticed a big drop in her typical late afternoon cravings. Only very occasionally will she have a small piece of the super dark chocolate her sister recommended, but never at night since it decreases the release of rejuvenating growth hormones essential for muscle growth, vitality and youthful looking skin. Michelle just loves the control she now has. When she feels like cheating, she looks at her before photograph and remembers how miserable she used to feel.

Questions to Contemplate

Now, how about you?

☐ How awesome might you look and feel 8 to 12 weeks from now?

☐ Why is it important for you to go for it now?

☐ What are you willing to stop doing and what will you start doing now to get and maintain the results you want?

☐ If you don't go for it, what might be the consequences and long-term prognosis for you?

☐ What benefits will you get from really going for it?

☐ What is your decision and goal? Irrevocable commitment?

☐ What do you need to believe and focus on to succeed?

☐ How can you best create or join a supportive environment?
Who will best be your accountability partner?

☐ For whom do you want to be an inspiration and role model?

Chapter 5

The Joy of Service

Daily, Scheduled Purpose Fulfillment

At the core of purpose fulfillment—daily habit number five—the joy of service is connected with our life's work. It is our opportunity to be abundantly fruitful in the service of ever-increasing numbers of people who need what we can do for them.

Action choice number five has the longest time allocation of all seven of the daily choices—from 7:45 am to 5:30 pm. This is the time each day when we focus on work, building systems, businesses, and passive income for the future, while fulfilling our purpose in life. We need to invest in our work instead of being a paycheck to paycheck employee in an unfulfilling job.

You may currently be a professional senior executive, middle or junior manager, or blue collar worker in someone's business. In many ways you are one of the lucky ones, and THE DAILY SEVEN system will work outstandingly well for you when it is followed with diligence.

However, there are pros and cons to being a salaried employee versus owning your own business. First of all, there is no real long-term guaranteed job security in any paycheck job as an employee. And people typically get paid about 20% of what management estimates they are worth as a fixed salary, leaving the company to profit from the other 80%. Furthermore, as employees, people only qualify for three tax benefits in the USA at the time of this writing.

On the other hand, as a business owner with employees, there are 103 tax benefits available, and those extra tax benefits make a very real difference when it comes to wealth creation and preservation. Having said that, you must also realize that a good job offers a steady income from which you can build great wealth if you practice effective asset allocation over a long enough period of time.

Doing Three Things Exceptionally Well

As a business owner or employee, you need to invest a significant amount of your time each working day to do three things exceptionally well:

1. Create and add profound value based on the needs of others and your core gifting. Use your gifts to serve them with outstanding excellence.

2. Research and invest in real value created by others and practice wise asset allocation, resource management and stewardship for passive income. Doing so will provide ever-increasing personal time for you to fulfill your purpose and to help others discover and fulfill theirs.

3. Take up the gauntlet on behalf of the poor, oppressed and underprivileged. Share with those in need.

Consider a balanced financial status with a solid mix of active, residual, passive, dividend and portfolio income, with well-located, in-demand real estate as a fundamental long-term cornerstone.

I believe in making money by building profitable businesses, networks, downlines, systems, programs and portfolios. Also add some carefully timed real estate speculation with particular focus on building an ever-growing real estate portfolio of rental real estate units for passive income.

Again, the question is how to begin working on your financial base. The following steps will give you a blueprint for laying a sure foundation in this area.

☐ Begin by first clarifying your purpose in life. Establish yourself in your niche and invest in increasing your knowledge and skills in this primary domain. Build ever-increasing ability, experience and qualifications, but above all, remember God's promise in the Scripture to us: "Seek first my righteousness and all good things will be added onto you."

☐ Study what works and what the best have done and are doing in your field. Remember, success in any endeavor leaves clues for others to follow. Be the best you can possibly be at what you do.

☐ Begin to build up residual and passive income in a network marketing business and/or by investing in a growing number of apartments, town houses, single-family homes, and office buildings to rent.

☐ Be wise and prepare in advance for the inevitable day when you, for whatever reason, will no longer be employed; and, as you see the day approaching, create a sound business plan for implementation.

☐ Plan and work to build a business by providing an above average quality experience, product and/or service for which there is a growing demand.

☐ Work to be better, faster, cheaper and nicer than your best competitors and aim for a 20% plus market share.

☐ Work to make a real and lasting difference in the lives of many people and build a loving home for your family. Why not dream and work towards a home with a breathtaking view on a mountaintop or a beautiful cabin in the woods? Whatever you do, make succeeding at home a top priority.

☐ Build a wise multi-disciplinary team around you for good counsel and be a proficient force on the team.

☐ Leverage other people's time, ideas, talents, experience, efforts and investment money respectfully to build assets.

Always be on the lookout for great ideas within your particular focus.

☐ Cultivate the art of using your banker's and investors' funds to acquire appreciating assets. Master the art and science of the wise non-use of personal cash to create and/or acquire appreciating positive income producing assets.

☐ Success in business, life and investing depends on a team effort. Develop your own ability to lead, sell and invest masterfully. You will be glad you did.

Reaping Abundantly

Know that you will ultimately reap an abundant reward if you will first:

☐ Fully develop your God-given gifts, market them and use them to benefit ever-increasing numbers of people.

☐ Develop ever-increasing and growing relationships and help enough people to get where they want to be in life.

☐ Ask the right questions and keep refining your ability to reach people.

☐ Communicate effectively and influence enough people with total integrity. Remember, *motives always matter*.

☐ Focus on building appreciating assets and reinvesting for compounded growth.

☐ Continuously work on being a better leader, sales negotiator, and investor. Practice adaptive learning and live with awareness and flexibility.

☐ Always do and give a little extra as a habit—extra effort, extra help, extra quality, a little extra gift, etc.

☐ Practice effective asset allocation with all income received and all existing assets. Keep your expenses on non-appreciating assets as low as practically possible. Look for ways to pay for them with pre-tax income. Talk to a knowledgeable CPA/tax advisor.

☐ Choose to avoid the lifestyle trap. Ignore what "the Jones" are doing—you do not need what they have to be a great person or even to be happy. The pursuit of the latest, biggest, best and fastest in everything is like drinking sea-water with lots of extra salt added—bottle after bottle it will only leave you with a greater thirst and eventually make you very sick.

Fundamental Asset Allocation Model

- 10% charitable giving
- 10% savings
- 20% or more to investing
- Live on 60% or less of your total expendable income.

If you have credit card and/or other short-term debt, use 20% or more of your income to eliminate your debt first.

Above all, keep your priorities straight—God, family, community, and self in that order. Never get this order of priorities mixed up. If you do, and you notice that you are off track, be quick to return to what you know deep down is the wiser path.

The price of success in business, relationships and life in general is high, but the price of failure is even higher.

Mark and Patricia—From Struggle to Victory

Mark and Patricia are smart, hard-working people; and as much as they do their best to progress in life, every time they make some good progress, something bad seems to happen. For every one step forward, they seem to take two steps backwards. They have certainly experienced their fair share of trials and tribulations just in the last year alone. Mark and Patricia's life so far has been full of struggles and living from paycheck to paycheck. This embarrassed Mark and made Patricia feel very insecure. They wondered what they needed to change in their lives. Their lives felt so out-of-balance.

Talking at night after a long day's work, they both confessed that they were not totally fulfilled in their careers. It was time for them to each ask some hard questions regarding their own beliefs, values, rules, habits and what they were really willing to do to create and enjoy a more rewarding and fulfilling life.

Both Mark and Patricia felt frustrated; they knew they could do much better but success continued to remain just a little out of reach. Patricia worked hard and had such a full load to deal with daily that, for most of the time, she ended up feeling overwhelmed. Regardless of how she tried to be more organized, some external factor almost always sabotaged her plans to stay in control of everything. There were just so many things to deal with at work, and with the kids, with Mark, her mother, the pets, community service and more. Patricia felt like she was needed by her family but yearned for more of a sense of meaning. She wanted to be important in more people's lives.

Mark and Patricia were not nearly at the level they wanted to be. Patricia always believed in Mark and secretly hoped and even prayed that he would get his act together and find something at which he could be truly outstanding. She wanted him to be happy, and more money would certainly also be very welcome. They had to find the strength to move beyond their procrastination, hesitation and fear of stepping out of their comfort zone.

They needed to realize that an opportunity for a better life would only come when they had the courage to take the risks required. One evening after dinner Mark gave Patricia a book dealing with how to find the "one thing" you were born to do, the thing that would make you feel fulfilled and become prosperous.

Mark and Patricia got so excited about the possibilities that they agreed to fly to a destination retreat offered by the author and some of his friends. For an entire weekend they focused on truly understanding their purpose in life and finding the confidence to follow it.

At the retreat they were asked the following questions:

☐ What is most important to you in life?

☐ What drives you—what is the primary emotion that you long deepest for?

☐ What are your greatest natural gifts and talents, your passionate burdens, the greatest obstacles you overcame, and your greatest frustrations?

☐ What are the needs, wants and desires of the people within your reach that you are most aware of?

☐ What disturbs your peace of mind and balance? What works best for you to restore your peace and balance?

☐ How do you want to be remembered?

They examined their own core beliefs, their current daily schedules, and their areas of strength as well as vital areas of neglect. They were forced to see the impact of their neglect in some areas and decided to make some very specific changes.

Together they talked about their finances, health, and relationship with God, their kids, and each other. They used the opportunity to talk about their emotions and how to better meet each other's needs. They discovered that they were long overdue to talk at this level of depth. In fact both Mark and Patricia agreed that talking to each other that weekend came just in time for them.

Mark realized he needed to romance his wife again, and Patricia was glad Mark could be so honest and open about his desires and fears. It confirmed so many things she sensed but felt uncomfortable to ask him. In fact they discovered they have even more in common than they ever realized. For example, Mark never realized how adventurous Patricia really was until then. They became totally in love again.

They both understood that what they were most looking for was a spiritual matter. They saw that there can be no accurate answer to life's greatest questions without a real relationship with the Creator of life. That weekend was above all else a spiritual awakening for them, one they would highly recommend. This retreat prompted them to ask the right and most important questions of themselves and each other. It was as if the retreat were part of their destiny. Looking back years later, they could clearly see how that weekend was a turning point in their lives.

Afterwards they enjoyed an enriched love life and were much more responsible with their money. However, the best result of the weekend proved to be that Mark found a deep certainty about what he wanted to do with the rest of his life. They continued working on their purpose quest questions they received at the retreat. One evening after their prayer time, Mark took the family dogs for a walk. He walked a little further than normal, alone in the still of the night, and suddenly he had his answer about his future, and with it, the faith to pursue it. He rushed back excitedly and told Patricia all about it. She knew he had been praying for quite some time, asking God to open his eyes to see his purpose and his ears to hear his calling, and to use him to solve a major problem for millions of people worldwide. What he was now telling her sounded like his prayers were answered.

Patricia could clearly see how it would benefit many people, and in the end, also enrich their lives both emotionally and financially beyond anything she ever dared to dream about. Patricia could also clearly see how her skills and talents were a perfect fit to help Mark bring this to market, and how their son could one day fit into the business. Patricia originally was hoping for her own independent career or business breakthrough, but this idea was better for all of them. It was the birth of a multi-intergenerational family business; she could not ask for more.

Mark and Patricia worked hard on the business and marketing plan. They had to take enormous but very calculated risks, and with the help of God they managed, even though at times it got unbelievably tough. At one time they almost went under and virtually lost it all. Throughout all their challenges, they both continued to declare their faith, gave a tithe to God's work, and held themselves to high personal standards.

From the beginning they were very careful with their money and reinvested most of their income back into the business instead of spending the profits on a bigger house, nice cars, clothes, jewelry, or luxurious travel, much as they were often tempted. They knew that to build an exceptional quality of life requires tremendous sacrifice, and they were willing to make that sacrifice. Mark and Patricia were glad they could set this example for their son and instill in him a life-long passionate commitment to contribute outstanding leadership and excellent service. The business progressed on a pre-planned schedule and in a mutually beneficial spirit, providing a great foundation for his future. He learned to dream big and to step up to the challenge.

Mark and Patricia's focus was on growing their business to serve ever-increasing numbers of people. They worked hard on quality and have remained fanatically obsessed with delivering outstanding quality and profound value. They also very carefully and systematically invested in well-located rental property units, mostly neglected and below market value apartments and townhouses, which they renovated. Today these units serve as steady income-producing assets for them, as well as affordable, decent housing for the community.

Mark now has a hobby of investing in old luxury cars, and wrist watches. He enjoys searching for a thirty-, forty- or fifty-year-old Bentley or a unique old watch, negotiating a great price on it. He has them restored to a pristine state and sells them at a good profit. He also has an old antique car that he fell in love with and just could not sell. He now rents it out, complete with a driver, as a wedding and special occasion vehicle. Patricia just loves being taken out on a date with Mark in it because it is so romantic.

Today, they have a very profitable and rapidly expanding business, and the future looks bright. They are now financially secure, well-protected with various trust accounts, a growing passive income from a solid real estate portfolio, and great additional residual income from their network marketing downline. After seven years in the business, this residual income alone was now more than enough to comfortably retire on.

Today they live in a great neighborhood, drive nice cars, have stylish clothes, enjoy luxurious travel, but all in moderation, and they understand that all these things are very temporary and of lesser importance in life. They both clearly remember the facilitator at the couples retreat asking them to drink a little seawater, while he explained that the quest for bigger, better, faster and the latest is just like drinking salted water—the more of it we drink, the thirstier we become and the sicker we get. This was a very valuable lesson, one they always reminded each other about.

Today they both know that true happiness is not to be found in the latest stuff, and that they were blessed so that they could be a blessing to others. They have seen so much suffering in their travels around the world, and both feel they simply could not close their eyes to all the pain and hunger around them. They understand that "from those to whom much is given, much is expected" and that if you cannot feed, clothe and shelter many, you can always help at least one. No matter how little you have, you can always give some to another person who needs it even more. Mark also enjoys teaching a class for entrepreneurs at a local college as a volunteer guest speaker and shares his views passionately with this group, as well as in the fellowship meetings for businessmen in their local church. Mark is now the immediate past president and current educational chairperson for their city's Young Entrepreneur's Club.

Their days are certainly very full but they totally love it. They would never have been able to imagine the outcome of their lives just a few years ago when they started out. God had been good to them, and they felt very deeply grateful, so much so that a year ago they started a charitable foundation. It has now largely became Patricia's full-time focus, and she enjoys every moment of it. She never worked this hard before but could not possibly be as fulfilled doing anything else. This was her destiny, of that she was sure.

For Mark and Patricia, work has become a form of worship—not that they worship their success, but they glorify God through what they do. They both say they believe that the master key to their success in life is their strong faith and deep spiritual base, which gives them the self-discipline, servant's heart and sound ethics to succeed. They also believe in tithing, which is giving 10% of their income to God's work. Mark and Patricia could clearly see God's hand in their lives, and as they acted on their faith and worked to help others, they experienced God's presence. They considered their lives to be extensions of God's work in the lives they were privileged to touch.

Their advice to others today is simple: First build a deep spiritual base with God at the center, think big because of Him, work diligently, be frugal, remain humble, and work to serve others in excellence for the honor of God, and tithe. As you become more and more blessed beyond anything you could even ask or think, be mindful to stay out of that bigger, better, faster, and latest trap—there are more important things to do with your money, things that are much more fulfilling.

Since Mark is such a driven businessman, he still continues to struggle a little in balancing his family and business life at times. He wants to be as successful at family life as he is at business. His peer group talks a lot about their need for a more balanced life, how they value balance, but for most of them it remains a rather elusive objective. He also has to work at being sensitive to other people's emotions and to have compassion on others, especially with underperformers. Like his buddies, he realizes that he needs to make his family an important focus in his life. The reality is that for their personality types, business tends to be their predominant focus. He has come a long way, though, and he is certainly more of a family man than he has ever been before.

Questions to Contemplate

☐ Who are you really? What are you really?

☐ Where do you come from?

☐ What is your purpose in life?

☐ Where do you want to go at the end of your life?

☐ What could represent the highest and best use of the lifetime you have left?

☐ What is most important to you in life now?

☐ What could your ten-million-dollar-plus breakthrough idea be?

☐ How could you best serve others and feel most fulfilled in the process?

☐ When are you going to take time out to dedicate at least one entire weekend to answer these questions and more in a unrushed manner, or at least make a start toward discovering your authentic answers?

☐ How would knowing these answer make you feel, and what would they enable you to do?

☐ What can you already be grateful for, right now?

Chapter 6

Sharing Ourselves

Daily, Scheduled Family and Friends Time

As a busy and ambitious international speaker, at times I have made the mistake of neglecting my family, and I deeply regret all that time lost. How about you? Time lost with them can never be regained, so it is extremely important to set a "non-negotiable family time." It should include at least one meal per day, most ideally dinner, as the central daily family time. Should the type of work you do make that impossible, ensure that at least one other meal is enjoyed together in an un-rushed manner—perhaps breakfast. With some effort, planning, preparation and discipline, it is certainly possible.

During your family meal, be sure to ask comfortable questions and not confrontational ones. Listen attentively, edify, and encourage support. Remember, *we all need more love than advice.* Be sure to make ample time for the entire family to enjoy times together. Pray and worship together, shop and prepare food together, eat together, walk together, play and watch movies together, enjoy holidays together; it is all part of the foundation for a happy, sustainable family life. Make time for each child individually to talk with them, read a story to them, and help them solve pressing issues in their lives.

Treat your spouse well with love, care, and respect. It is vital that your children have this nurturing example for their overall development and sense of security. Be aware of your choice of words, voice tonality and body language. Hug your spouse and children often and shower them with sweet words. Build fond memories to last a lifetime,

Please stop your workaholic habits. If you cannot or do not make enough money working from 7:45 in the morning to 5:30 in the afternoon, then there is a problem that another two or three hours a day of work will not solve. If your mobile phone has the capability, preset it to automatically switch off at 7:00 pm at night and switch automatically back on again at 7:00 am each day.

Downscale. Simplify your life if you must, but do all you can to not lose what is most precious. If you already have done destructive things, do all you can to rebuild your family life the best you can with whatever is left.

Don't destroy your family life with workaholism, rules that are too strict, pettiness, or overcritical behavior. That's something we all need to remember. Be much more accepting. Don't let your spouse or children feel that they are only lovable or have value if they succeed in a career, at school or in sports. There is much more to life!

Time passes swiftly and lost time can never be regained. Make the most of today with your loved ones and restructure your life to enjoy more nurturing family time. Play more, love more, and share more. You will be glad you did! If you live alone, call your loved ones regularly or at least allocate time to e-mail or text message them. Spend some time with special friends for fellowship and fun social interaction. If you feel lonely, try doing some volunteer work. Life is to be enjoyed.

Having dinner with your family most nights is a great start, but how about having one night a week, e.g. Friday, Saturday or Sunday night as a non-negotiable family fun night, exclusively for the entire family together? How about adding Wednesday night to talk together, plan a retreat or vacation for the entire family together, budget together, play word quizzes or other educational board games together. In other words, do something everyone can enjoy together. You could also have a family prayer meeting once a week for the entire family to read scripture together, discuss and pray together.

Let your kids see you making a list of 100 things to give, do, see, and share before you pass on. Let them see you tick off some big life adventures from your list. Let them see you dream big, for example, go on a hot air balloon safari in east Africa, hike the foothills of the Himalayas, walk with elephants in Malawi, cruise down the Amazon, mush in Alaska, or fish or horseback ride in Montana.

Let your kids see you practice kindness and charity—anonymous giving, charitable volunteer service, and philanthropic giving. Let them watch you give old clothes and books, with big dollar bills tucked in the pockets and between the pages, to charitable shelters and street people.

Let them see you go to church, pray before you eat, wash your car, volunteer and serve in your community, donate to disaster funds and nature conservation. Let them see you read good books, exercise, budget, demonstrate and express love, open doors for others, garden and clean and fix things, buy and eat healthy foods. That is practical parenting at its best.

Go camping with your family, discover new things and new places together, workout and play some sports together. Having casual fun is good for families. Don't let your time together just be going to movies and eating out, although that is good and has its place at times. But there is so much more to life.

Be the one in your extended family to start an annual family retreat tradition. Inspire and guide everyone to join you in the creation of a defined, written and shared family identity statement, family purpose statement, and family code-of-conduct. Honor the elderly family members by asking them to tell the stories of their lives and the stories of their parents and their parents' lives, so that the family tribal stories and God's hand in your ancestors' lives may be recognized and honored.

Families who do this have deep roots and a sense of belonging. Give your kids this gift at a family retreat and build a stone memorial with family touchstones representing major family events, symbols of God's love and care in your family history.

Bob and Nicole—a Family Transformation

Bob and Nicole are both hard-working people. Nicole is attractive, smart and well-educated. She loved the challenges of her job but she had to commute a total of almost three hours every day and typically arrived home just a little before seven, stressed out, hyped up and exhausted. The last thing she felt like doing was making decisions about what to cook for dinner. She was at the breaking point and desperate for a way out. She wanted evenings at home with her family to be fun, light and relaxed. She wanted a deeper emotional connection, a positive pleasant atmosphere, and intimacy with Bob.

Bob, a graphic designer, an intellectual and sensitive person, works from home. He began work in their home office just before seven in the morning and worked straight through with almost no breaks until just before seven at night when Nicole returned from work. He too would be mentally exhausted from a long day of all-out effort to build a better quality of life for them, and he was in no mood for household chores. Nicole was often in a bad mood between seven and nine at night. She was very impatient and would get into bad moods very easily, making her hard to be around at times, wonderful as she was at other times. Her three teenaged kids were self-admittedly lazy, spoiled and messy. The tension in the family increased day by day. She felt there must be more to life than just work and home responsibilities. Nicole was a creative, artistic person, and she craved more fun, free time and adventure in her life.

Nicole was becoming increasingly depressed and started to escape by reading novel after novel, feeling there must be more to life. Bob could see her struggle; he loved Nicole and felt sorry for her. He really wanted to help her find more balance in her life and give her the space and support she needed to reach her full potential in her career. He could clearly see how her work drained her. In her managerial capacity she had to take care of everyone and everything and simply did not have the energy left to do the same thing at home as well. Nicole's demanding work life, long hours of commuting and demands from the kids resulted in her neglecting her relationship with Bob, her own personal growth, and her peace and joy. Bob felt he had to find a way to help her more. Bob really understood Nicole's needs, and he was willing to do whatever it took to help her.

Bob, a former corporate executive, was recovering from adrenal gland depletion, or more likely burnout and a recent retrenchment that pulled heavy on his emotions, especially his self-esteem and sense of worth. Like so many men, he was captive to the false belief that it was his work and ability to earn that made him a real man.

Their family life was chaotic; the kids' rooms, bathroom and kitchen a constant mess; and the kids seemed not to care much about how much it upset Nicole. Bob, a more structured and disciplined person, battled with this problem. He knew there must be a better way to live.

Bob was being lured back into the rat race with a very promising job offer as marketing director, and possibly even managing director, of a dynamically expanding business with international offices worldwide. This steady income, although not very high initially, would be a welcome relief, but it would mean occasional late night meetings, travel and a heavy work load all taking time away from his family at a time when Nicole was desperate for more support. Bob was already working for this new corporation part-time from home, setting things up for his official integration into the group. Between that work and his current home-based business, his days were very full and demanding. This part-time job quickly became more like a full-time job. Bob and Nicole both felt like they were stuck in the rat race to make ends meet, leaving both of them exhausted, difficult to be with, and arguing about who should have gone to the grocery store, or cleaned or cooked. They loved each other, but the fighting hurt both of them so much.

This was their second marriage each. Nicole grew up in a house where her father cooked almost all the meals, and her former husband cooked most of them too. Bob, however, grew up seeing his mother, a hard-working entrepreneur, cook all the meals. And he came from a relationship where his former wife cooked eighty percent of the meals. Both Nicole and Bob were good cooks, but during the years when Nicole and the kids were on their own, they had gotten into the habit of eating out most nights. Nicole had found it easier to do than to cook and clean when she was so tired. Now Nicole seemed to expect Bob to do most, if not all the cooking, and that did not fit his model of how things should be. They needed to clarify their roles.

Bob really believed in the institution of a family dinner and felt that it was a great waste of money and time to eat out so often. He felt their money could be put to better use for their future, and waiting in line at restaurants that do not take reservations was an unpleasant waste of time.

Bob made great winter soups and fantastic summer salads; he also enjoyed barbequing, but felt he was not ready for the task of having full-time responsibility for dinners and keeping the kitchen clean. It seemed like such a thankless task, and he had a new career to build. The kids especially seemed to take things for granted and to carelessly make messes, knowing someone else would clean up after them. Bob was not willing to be this housekeeper; he was a career-oriented person. What really drove him crazy was when he had a headache and walked into the kitchen after almost 12 hours of detailed computer work to find the television blaring rap music, news of war, natural disasters, crimes, or violent movies from the adjoining room. When he asked the kids to please turn it down while he cooked and cleaned, they ignored his request and pretended it was absurd to even think the TV should not be so loud. If it were not for the noise, he would have been willing to spend more time in the kitchen. Bob wanted a family life where the home environment was much more tranquil, restful and spiritual, a place to recover and recuperate. He needed to find a sanctuary to escape to, so the problem drove him back into the office at night, starting a whole new destructive pattern.

During his previous career in the corporate world, Bob missed many family meals, something he regretted deeply. To him, no job would ever be worth it again. He was willing to work hard from early in the morning until 6:00 pm or so. He maintained that married corporate people who could consistently not earn enough working from seven or eight in the morning to six at night, are either ineffective, greedy, selfishly ambitious, or simply have their priorities messed up. He fully understood that there would be special occasions when there was a need to work late into the night, but unless someone was a startup entrepreneur, he felt they should be the exception not the norm. Bob felt that married people with children should be back home together for dinner by the very latest 8:00 pm, and ideally much earlier, depending on the age of the kids. Bob and Nicole both wanted more order and balance in their lives. They had to find a workable solution and build in some agreed upon escapism for both of them without neglecting the kids and/or each other.

Nicole wanted to resign from her demanding job, move to a less expensive part of the country, closer to her natural family support team. She hoped Bob could earn more, so that she could be a stay-at-home mom again. The kids had gotten used to her being at home, and she felt they needed her there again. Bob wanted her not to work at all or, at the very most, only half days and at something she really wanted to do. Right now that would not be easy. He needed to have this new job for a few seasons at least; in fact, he was looking to make it a long-term focus and could not move at this time. Bob could also see Nicole's need for more family support and time with her children. What could their solution possibly be?

Something had to change and it had to change fast, but could they really manage it? Bob believed they could, and prayed for God's direction.

Nicole and Bob agreed that they would make being home by 6:30 pm at the latest for a family dinner by 7:00, an agreed upon standard. Bob would cook Mondays, and Nicole would cook on Tuesdays. Wednesdays and Thursdays they would cook together, as well as on Sundays. On Fridays they would get carry out, taking turns picking it up. On Saturdays they would either go to a restaurant to eat out, or Bob would make a barbeque, and they would eat leftovers on Sunday. Bob already made breakfast most of the time and packed Nicole a beautiful lunch to take to work when he was not traveling. He knew that deep down Nicole just wanted to be taken care of, and he did love spoiling her.

Bob did not want the kids to grow up lazy, and being their cleaning and cooking maid did not fit his identity. They now set a rule that the kids had to set the table every night, and after the meal each one would scrape their own plate, rinse it and place it in the dishwasher. Pots, pans, and serving plates would be cleaned by Bob and Nicole. Bob would mostly say grace before their meals, but the opportunity would be open for anyone to do so, and at Sunday supper Bob would also read some Scripture. The kids would also receive a reasonable and appropriate weekly allowance for helping with additional chores. Failing to fulfill their end of the bargain meant a reduction of 10% in their allowance each time. They were also strongly encouraged to give 10%

percent each week at church and to save 10% responsibly. Nicole and Bob felt that these were wise character habits they wanted their kids to grow up with.
On Saturdays they went food shopping for the week, and on Wednesdays, they took turns resupplying the household with fresh bread, milk and fruit from the local store.

Nicole and Bob also agreed that Sunday nights were to be dedicated family nights, set aside exclusively for family time. They felt this system gave them the best possible chance to reduce stress in the family and raise their kids as best they could. It would not necessarily be easy but the alternative would be much harder.

For the most part, their plan worked out very well, although life is not perfect and challenges did occur. The system did fail at times, but at least there was a basis of agreement from which to work. In fact they wished they had started being a bit more structured, planned and organized sooner since it certainly made life a lot less stressful.

All of them began to love their family dinner time together at the table with no television or interfering phone calls. It became a cornerstone of their family relationship and a major anchor keeping them all connected. Today they are very glad they made this decision and held themselves to it.

Bob and Nicole also agreed that before they began this new plan, it would be good to go on a family retreat with the kids to help them draw closer to one another. They decided to go camping somewhere for a weekend to create a strong family identity, a family purpose statement and an agreed upon code of conduct. They decided not to settle for a chaotic family life when they could create and enjoy the life of their dreams. They also felt the family retreat would give the kids a better sense of belonging and deeper roots for when the storms of life came their way.

Bob had the idea for them all to collect some river stones during their trip. At the campfires they shared family stories, lessons learned, and all their hopes, dreams and aspirations. They passed a stone around the circle, and each one who held the stone had the opportunity to speak from the heart, completely and totally uninterrupted. On their return home they used the big stones in a prominent spot in their garden to build a memorial reminding them of their special weekend and commitment to each other, and of the love and connection they shared. It would be a monument to the history of their family. It was Bob and Nicole's intention that their children's children would one day see the stones piled up high and ask about it, and that their children would tell the family stories, and testify of God's love, goodness and provision. It was their prayer that it would become a powerful experience and tradition in their family.

This was great family leadership at its practical best and was a way to touch their children again in the future. Bob also used some of the smaller stones to build a miniature memorial on a piece of wood to keep on his desk in his new corporate office, and he always carried one small, smooth touch stone in his suit pocket on his business travels away from home.

Nicole wondered what else they could do as a family to stay and grow together. On a very emotional level this really mattered deeply to her. She thought that perhaps they could pray more together. Bob was fulfilling his role as spiritual head of the household reasonably well, but she needed to support and encourage him a little more in this area, which she did. Their life was still very far from perfect, but it certainly was a lot better.

Bob still saw a need for Nicole to have more downtime for fun, variety and relaxation. He decided to encourage her to take one night a week completely off when he would take care of dinner, sign the kids' homework and do everything else that was needed. It would be her night to do whatever she wanted—go to sleep early, read a book uninterrupted, or go for a manicure. Nicole could socialize with friends, pursue a hobby, attend a Pilates class, or anything else she believed would be fun, fulfilling and satisfying for her. She clearly needed this sense of freedom, and he was willing to let her have it. He trusted her to make wise and mature choices. Bob also decided to make home life as pleasant and happy as possible for Nicole so that time at home would eventually become Nicole's first choice. He trusted that as her spirit matured, Nicole would be more at peace with life. For now Bob realized he had to be more flexible and supportive.

Ultimately they would get away into a country setting with a slower pace and simpler lifestyle. That was their goal, but for a time they would press on, with an agreed upon plan that could work.

Questions to Contemplate

☐ What can you do to free your spouse from some of her/his burdens?

☐ How important is your family to you and why?

☐ What do you want to teach your children by example and what character traits and habits do you feel necessary to instill in them?

☐ How can better planning, organizing and role clarity reduce stress in your household?

☐ What will you absolutely do to ensure a calm, loving, orderly family dinner at 7:00 pm or earlier as many nights as possible?

☐ What schedule, menu plan and shopping list would work best for your entire family?

☐ What rules, regulations, rewards and penalties will ensure success in your household?

☐ What would be the short term and long term consequences of not making family dinners a priority? Why do you need to get this handled now?

☐ What did you pick up from this story that you can implement immediately in your family life?

Chapter 7

Filling the Well

Daily, Scheduled Personal Quiet Time

The practice of having personal quiet time, or in other words "filling the well," is a vital choice to make each day. Plan this for the end of your day. For dad it can be meditative evening walks with the family dog or 30 minutes of solitude on the porch, deck or balcony. For mom it could be 30 minutes alone in a warm bath, perhaps with some floating rose petals, oil and soft candlelight. Make this time non-negotiable; make it a special time to take outstanding care of yourself, to cleanse, relax and restore. Be inspired and encouraged to create in your home or garden a special place where you can feel renewed.

You also need to take care of your spiritual side. If you draw THE DAILY SEVEN in a circle, connecting the beginning and the end, you will see the need to use a portion of this time (extend the time as needed) for prayer to give gratitude to God and for reflective journaling and a little creative writing if creative inspirational thoughts whisper in your mind and heart. This time is very important. Please do not neglect it—it will help to keep you centered and connected to God's purposes for you.

And then, before a well-deserved and good night's sleep, be close, loving and intimate with your spouse. Know what your partner values and do for her/him what she/he needs most. Plan, schedule, and honor regular time out together as it is vital for high and sustained productivity.

Make time to rest, not because you are a slacker, but because of your high personal commitment to quality contributions in your sphere of influence and responsibility. Take great care of yourself so that you have the health and energy to take great care of others, and so that you may be more fun to be with. Everyone around you will happier.

Enjoy time to rest and truly relax to calm and balance your central nervous system, detoxify your mind and body, regenerate your creativity, replenish your enthusiasm, and rebuild your energy supply.

Rediscover what gives you pleasure and what centers and balances you best and then make a regular time to enjoy more of it. Your reward will be a much greater quality of life and greatly increased ability to cope and even compete at high levels of demand.

Daniel—The Power of Silence

Daniel is an obsessively self-driven and highly focused person who does things with great passion and vigor, a very animated, high energy go-getter, who like many of his peers struggled to maintain real balance between family and his business life.

He too runs the risk of high blood pressure and, as much as he believes in daily exercise, also struggles to maintain his own extraordinarily high standards of exercise when he travels on business. The one great thing about travel though is that it gives him more time alone at night in his hotel room to reflect, pray, journal his thoughts, and experience the power of silence and solitude.

During his days he has so many demands on his attention and so much activity in his life that he needs the other side—the solitude and stillness.

At night after supper at home, quietness in the house is important to him, especially after nine at night. He feels it is important for everyone to have thirty minutes or more of personal quiet time just to be still. On nights when that appears to be an elusive goal, he takes the dog out for a half hour, walking slowly and prayerfully. Of paramount importance to him, though, is to have enough quietness in the bedroom or study to sit and pray for at least fifteen to twenty minutes undisturbed.

When he travels, Daniel typically stays in smaller high-end hotels, asking well in advance for a quiet room. After calling his family to talk with his wife and each of the kids individually, he usually eats a light meal, goes for a brisk walk—one of the best exercises he finds after long flights and business meetings—and then retreats to his room where he takes his shoes off, loosens up, and does stretching exercises for 15 or more minutes.

Afterwards he sits quietly for thirty to forty minutes or more at a time, with a relaxed yet upright and balanced posture and his chin slightly tucked in, relaxing all his muscles, especially the many tiny little muscles in his face and around his jaw and mouth. At home most of the time, he has only about fifteen to thirty minutes available for this at night, but it leaves him very calm, relaxed and at peace.

As he prays, he gives thanks for everything he loves and values in his life. He prays for his family, for his friends, for his staff, and clients and suppliers—each one by name and in significant detail, asking God to protect them, bless them and favor them richly. He often writes these prayers out as he prays them. He also prays for the areas in the world where there is great suffering, for the nation and for more wisdom among all the leaders. He prays that God will use him more and more to be a blessing in the lives of others.

Often he reads something deeply profound, wise and valuable. He selects the core statement and writes it down. He has found that this significantly increases his own ability to communicate in powerful and memorable ways.

Afterwards he will typically take a long hot bath with a little relaxing natural aromatherapy oil and sleep soundly. He has found that this routine prepares him well to wake up totally refreshed.

Questions to Contemplate

☐ How can you best create for yourself a special quiet sanctuary to retreat to for silence and for time with God?

☐ How can you best begin with short prayers and meditations, and progress from there?

☐ How will you begin to incorporate these ideas into your daily life?

And now my friend—may I call you friend—after you have read my entire system for building a better life and know my heart so well, may I please ask you, if you unexpectedly passed away tonight, where would your soul spend eternity? If you don't know and want to be sure, I would like to invite you to go to my website (see the last page of this book for the address) and click on "A Personal Matter" and allow me the privilege to talk to you one-on-one for a few minutes and to guide you in a simple prayer that will give you total certainty. Today is the day and now is the time, don't listen to your head, listen to your heart and do it now.

THE DAILY SEVEN SUGGESTED TIME ALLOCATIONS

D1 – The Call of Destiny
Daily, Scheduled Spiritual Enrichment
5:00 am

D2 – The Developed Mind
Daily, Scheduled Mental Development
5:30 am

D3 – The Physically Conditioned Body
Daily, Scheduled Physical Conditioning
6:00 am

D4 - Intelligent Nutrition
Daily, Scheduled Portion-Controlled Nutrition
7:00, 10:00, 12:30, 3:00, 7:00. 9:00

D5 – The Joy of Work
Daily, Scheduled Purpose Fulfillment
7:45 am – 5:30 pm

D6 – Sharing Ourselves
Daily, Scheduled Family/Friends Time
7:00 – 9:00 pm

D7 – Filling the Well
Daily, Scheduled Personal Quiet Time
9:00 – 10:00 pm

Note: Feel free to adjust these times somewhat as your own life realities dictate, to ensure you will be able to follow the system consistently.

Remember the real power of THE DAILY SEVEN is not in doing one of them or even some of them very well, *the greatest power is only generated by doing all seven with outstanding excellence.* That is when you give yourself the best possible chance of a deeply satisfying life of great meaning, purpose, contribution, and yes, achievement. The power is in the synergistic value of all seven working together, each supporting and affecting all the others in very real and powerful ways.

Important: To get the greatest benefit from this book and system, we suggest you give between one and twelve friends each a copy of this book. Create a forum for a small group meeting once a week. Meet for a minimum of seven weeks and or go on a weekend retreat specifically to work through this book together. Diligently meet at a regular time to discuss one chapter each of THE DAILY SEVEN and to fellowship. Reflect on your experience in that area, encourage each other, hold each other to a high standard, and be accountable to each other in a loving, supportive way.

Who could you invite, and in whose life can you be a godly influence? Whose influence and support do you need?

Will you rise up as a leader and friend and do this, or will you shrink from the challenge? I believe you can do it. Go for it, and the power will be there as it always is where two or more are gathered.

PART TWO

PROFIT IN EXCELLENCE

You don't have to
lose your family, health,
or soul on your way
to success!

Chapter 8

Breakthrough to Excellence

In this section we will deal with significantly increasing your effectiveness and income within the bigger framework of balancing every vital area of your life.

The following is a catalytic action plan for you to reach the next level of professional excellence or to improve any other area of your life. If you want a breakthrough, here is what you need to do.

1. Get Real, Get Upset, Get a Vision.

Decide what matters and know exactly why and how it matters to God, you and others.

Get Real: Is there an area of your life with which you are not satisfied? Do not settle for less than excellence. Get real about where you are in this area of your life. What is the problem area costing you—emotionally, spiritually, mentally, physically, financially? What pain has it brought you in the past and what will it cost you in the future?

Get Upset: Let your pain fuel you with inspirational discontent and ambitious aspiration, and ignite in you an unstoppable need to change. In your pain seek God and ask for His forgiveness, wisdom and guidance.

Get a Vision: Ask for a new vision for this area of your life. Expect a divine revelation. Let go of the failures of yesterday while holding onto the lessons that you learned from them. Out of your personal pain, a new and greater thing for your life will be forged. Looking back you will understand how that was used to bring you to a new and better place in life.

2. Identify your past self-limiting and destructive patterns.

What is there in your character, habits and lifestyle that are at the root cause of your pain, frustration and blockage? What is it that you have been doing that you simply should never do again? What must stop now? Identify your weaknesses and admit them.

Journal your pain, anger or shame, prayerfully surrender it to God, and begin today to make a new set of choices to become a new you.

In your business, what are the blinders, distractions, processes, relationships, and outdated beliefs and dogmas that limit you? Identify your fears, self-doubts, bad habits, unrestrained and ungodly conduct, and self-esteem eroding patterns.

Know that fear exists powerfully where there is inadequate faith in God, inadequate love, knowledge, skill, preparation, support and truth.

3. Gain new perspectives and redefine what is possible for you.

Get clarity and encourage your spirit with new, powerful and emotive words. Define accurately what and who you truly are, and redefine what you are capable of accomplishing. Create a new code of conduct at a higher standard, write it down, and begin to live it, making no compromises. Read it out loud each morning.

Set a clear, specific goal that is aligned with your purpose and desires. Get clear on what it is that you want. Decide and commit it in writing. Have a big enough personal reason for wanting it. This is vital. Declare out loud the goal you most want to achieve and know exactly why you want it.

Gain new perspective and enjoy new experiences. Realize that your spirit is greater than your current circumstances and conditions. You are capable of so much more.

You need to set higher spiritual, mental, emotional, physical and financial standards. The standards you set as non-negotiable minimum and the standards you settle for largely determine the level at which we get to work, play and live.

4. Find godly role models, prayer partners, coaches, mentors, an accountability group, an advisory board and support group.

Those who are the best in their field all have coaches, mentors and a support team—how about you? Learn from the best. Emulate and improve on their winning strategies. Build around you a multi-disciplinary advisory board and be on one. Who will/can invest in you? Who can be your best technical advisors and helpers? Who can help you do the actual work at a world-class level? How can you best use leverage and teach others to do what you do?

5. Get a system and put yourself on a schedule.

Raise your standards and refuse to settle for less than excellence in your life. Do not let thoughts of short-term pain stop you from doing what you know you must do. Dare to be one of the very best! Make your work a form of worship.

Dream greater dreams for yourself and others. Do the work of your heart with all your heart. Fulfill your roles and purpose in excellence. Develop a detailed plan and work diligently on a time-protected schedule while ensuring adequate family time. Ultimately live your purpose, and you will discover the enormous joy that comes from serving with excellence. Be exceptionally excellent and give all thanks to God.

Consider taking the following steps:

☐ Take control over your personal cash flow—learn how to have money work for you.

☐ Don't just accumulate liabilities, acquire appreciating assets.
☐ Build and use systems and checklists.
☐ Invest more in your own knowledge and skills, study how to lead, sell, build businesses and brands, raise capital, establish a family trust and a charitable foundation.
☐ Learn how to become a greater leader and better sales negotiator; learn how to build a passive income portfolio in real estate.
☐ Build a balanced and diversified investment portfolio with real estate as your primary vehicle and cornerstone. Always be mindful of the direction of the market.
☐ Work daily to be the best you can be, but do not neglect your spirit, family and health in the process. No success is worth it. Remember, the secret is balanced focus.
☐ Dare to be great and to give all thanks to God.

Ask yourself the following questions:
☐ Will what I do have an impact on the great cities on the edges of the earth?
☐ Will I continue to live in the hearts of many people long after I have gone?
☐ How can I be part of the boom in the wellness industry and retirement real estate?
☐ Which network-marketing group will I best fit into and how can I build an ever-expanding downline and optimize the tax benefits of business ownership now?
☐ How can I acquire the greatest future value real estate bargain today?
☐ How can I acquire it without much money?
☐ How can I best serve a growing need in the global market?

- ☐ How can I deliver increasing value at a lower cost to the consumer?
- ☐ How can I reach additional markets?

Remember that you have the innate ability to meet all your loved ones needs. Believe it and go for it. Do your part and God will do His.

You still have the beautiful gift of life, an abundant opportunity and an unknown numbered amount of tomorrows left. Believe in possibilities; take nothing for granted. Express and demonstrate gratitude. Help others to bring their light to the world.

6. Seek Feedback

Seek mature feedback with humility, dignity and respect. Monitor, log, measure, analyze, evaluate, and counsel.

7. Practice Adaptive Learning

Seek corrective support and remain flexible in your strategies. Keep on refining them. Commit yourself to lifelong adaptive learning and constant never-ending improvement. Persist with flexibility.

Begin what you can right now. Head confidently towards fulfilling your dreams and stay committed. Yes, your faith will be tested but keep your faith strong. Remember that you are important, you are significant, and you are needed. Right now there are certainly people within your reach who need what you can do. Go find them; they are waiting for your call.

We need each other and we need the gifts that each one is predestined to share. We need the love, talents, potential, business, contacts and contribution of each other. Always be a part of those who give. Live your purpose!

Chapter 9

Called to Lead

Organizations and groups worldwide succeed and fail largely because of their leadership. Quality leadership is one of the single most vital factors for the effectiveness and survival of any business, organization, group or family.

Here is a proven five-step model that can make you a much-loved, respected and outstanding leader. Dare to be a godly leader, demonstrate spirituality in the workplace, and promote the philosophy of work as a form of worship.

1a. **PREPARE YOUR HEART** prayerfully, then walk slowly among your people. Ask great questions and teach your people to ask great questions.

Think of John F. Kennedy who said, "Ask not what your country can do for you, but what you can do for your country."

Get to know the hearts of your people, get to know their strengths and weaknesses, their hopes, dreams and aspirations, and their everyday realities.

Build sincere relationships with them and ask questions such as, "What is most important to you?" "What is it that your heart yearns and aches for?" "What if it is possible for you to…?" Ask them what they think on a variety of subjects. Listen attentively to their answers so that you may become relevant in their lives.

Managers Speak to People's Heads; Leaders Speak to People's Hearts.

1b. **SPEAK INTO THEIR HEARTS** and stir up their gifts. Sincerely say "I believe in you, I want you to succeed, and I will help you to succeed."

2a. **COMMUNICATE A COMPELLING VISION** with certainty, authenticity, and confidence.

Speak certainty to the people. Show them what is in it for them. Spend time with each and every key individual, and as many others as possible, to ensure buy-in, commitment, and role clarity. Edify and praise them publicly and say "John/Mary I depend on you to…." Be explicitly clear in your request of a specific, doable-with-effort outcome.

2b. **EQUIP AND TRAIN YOUR TEAM FOR SUCCESS**; train and retrain continually. Plan, rehearse, drill, execute, debrief, coach and repeat. Always remember, proper preparation prevents poor performance; and a casual approach leads to casualties.

Be very careful and strict in the selection of people. Ensure that their values and core beliefs are aligned with your corporate culture, mission and objectives. Remember that identity precedes behavior, and that a high, healthy self-esteem leads to high performance. Build high self-esteem.

3. **LEAD BY EXAMPLE**. Be an inspiring and highly proficient role model. Be a godly influence insofar as possible; hold yourself to a higher standard. Give 100%. Always shoulder more than your fair share of the load. Live with total honesty and build a "Get the Job Done With Outstanding Excellence" culture by example.

Do what is difficult. If a path is easy it is probably not worth taking. Continually taking the path of least resistance results in a life of neglect and destruction. If you are easy on yourself, life will be hard on you; and, if you are hard on yourself, life will be easy on you. To a large extent the same is true in raising children. A certain amount of discipline and order is vital and must be learned at home first, to set one's children up for success outside the safety and comfort of home. Endeavor to live as best you can by a carefully chosen code of conduct, summarized in a personal creed or motto.

4. **BE A GREAT MENTOR** and a coach, and make sure you have some for yourself as well.

On the job, life experience alongside an experienced worker and/or coach is the best kind of training. Assimilated and role-play training is also valuable.

Look continually for good performance. Be quick to point it out, especially when it is above standard performance.

5. **SET UP BEST-IN-THE-BUSINESS SYSTEMS**. True professionals, the best of the best, all use systems, checklists and drills, with total focus, commitment and diligence, along with a touch of flexibility in truly unique and extreme situations only. Reward the use of systems and checklists with recognition. Publicly recognize and reward excellence, recognize both compliance and initiative, and place the emphasis on whichever you need more of at the time and in the future. Be generous with rewards and lavish with sincere recognition and praise when they are earned. Focus on merit and contribution. Recognize all sincere effort and contributions. Acknowledge and celebrate all-out efforts that set new standards of technical, managerial and/or service excellence, and which result in profitable success. Recognize and support both developed and developing talent.

If you ever have to take corrective action, it means your systems and checklists failed to prevent the problem. Adjust your systems wisely. Take absolutely no pride or pleasure in your ability to punish; instead, avoid it. Have mercy. The power to forgive and grant mercy is true power. When you absolutely have to discipline and punish, awe them with intensity, but always in proportion to the issues at hand. Unless there is sincere regret, people will most likely not change their behavior in the absence of adequate consequences. Pain is indeed the precursor to human change.

Lead decisively; but most importantly, lead in excellence and love in service of those you lead.

Remember that people, including one's children, need more love and better examples more than they need advice. Most people are under-loved. Love them and they will love you for it. Choose to be deeply interested in others and in helping them.

May I also suggest that you pray for your people and document your prayers for each individual you pray for in a prayer journal. Pray for all your key people, suppliers, clients, and investors. Pray for their benefit, good health and prosperity.

How much action can you get yourself and others to take? This is a key question in effective leadership that gets things done.

Chapter 10

Watch With Whom You Fellowship

Achievers worldwide believe in the power of association, i.e. that we become like the company we keep. How about you—what do you believe?

☐ With whom do you invest most of your time? Are they worth emulating? Will you be more fulfilled and satisfied when you are more like them or less?

☐ What kind of words do they use and in what context? What do they do with their time? Do they waste theirs? If so, then know that they will also waste yours.

☐ What do they read and attend and think about most and encourage you to do likewise? Will it put you on a higher path or lower path? Does it make you a better person or not? What does your heart tell you?

☐ What is their contribution to the world? Do they make a difference?

☐ Where do they get the majority of their income from—active, dividend, portfolio, residual or passive income?

☐ What are their hopes, dreams and aspirations?

☐ What is their core philosophy of life? What do they value? What do they believe? Look at character first, not personality.

☐ What and who influences them and who do they have influence with?

☐ What will more time with them make you become?

☐ Analyze your appointment book and be conscious of how the people with whom you most associate impact your thinking, decisions and future.

☐ Be careful and very selective with whom you invest time. Associate with the best, however, never become too big, proud or arrogant not to make time for people who are less accomplished. Your humility, teaching, and compassionate assistance is vital for them, and even more so for you. Make time for those who need your help, especially those who are at the lowest levels of society and in your organizations, with love, dignity, care and respect.

Chapter 11

$ell and Grow Rich

In business what ultimately matters most is cash flow. Cash flow is the oxygen in the lifeblood of any organization. Unless more sales are made, no organization can grow; and unless sales are continually made, no organization can survive for long.

The art of selling is fundamentally the art of asking great questions and can be learned and mastered. Ultimately we all sell something, whether it is our time, ideas, skills, a product or service experience. The better we are at it, the more money we can make.

Here are six fundamental keys to master.

1. **PREPARATION**

   a. Build an indomitable self-image, on a healthy

foundation of self-esteem.

b. Recall, list and celebrate your past achievements.

c. List all your gifts and finest qualities; attend skill set and self-esteem building seminars.

d. Set a compelling goal and some exciting milestone objectives. Make the milestone objectives small, easy-to-achieve actions. List them and tick them off as you accomplish them to create a sense of progress.

e. Dress for success. Be immaculately groomed and dress appropriately. Look like a leader. Invest in high quality suit(s), high quality business shirts/blouses, good shoes, a neat professional briefcase, a quality pen, neat notebook and notepad, a quality watch, etc. For men perhaps a dark navy blue, black or charcoal gray suit, perhaps with a pinstripe. A crisp white-collar shirt, black belt/suspenders, black shoes, black socks, black briefcase, black quality day planner, black/gold pen and a red, maroon, navy blue, gold or black necktie for the ultimate corporate/professional success looks. For ladies it should be very similar—a business suit, white blouse and black and gold accessories.

f. Script and list daily. Begin each workday by investing a few minutes each morning writing out various ways to ask questions, how to best present your offer, and how to best overcome objections and ask more "moving forward" questions. Be a student of masterful word patterns. What would be the most effective, impactful or memorable way to ask or say something?

g. Make a daily list of prospects to call, and call them the very same day. Watch and listen to the world's greatest communicators and be conscious of words, word structures and communication patterns that you could integrate into your own communication.

h. Prepare all your samples well in advance and in a totally organized manner. This will not only give you a more professional edge but also boost your own confidence.

Commit to excellent preparation and winning habits, and you will become the winner you plan to be. It is absolutely vital to have a specific and structured sales presentation pre-planned as a guideline to use with flexibility. If your sales presentation plan sounds like a scripted plan, it is because it is not adequately rehearsed and integrated into your thinking.

Check to see if your sentences are too long. Work at keeping them brief and remain flexible. Script multiple options for the same ideas to give you more flexibility. Be a credible expert with a quality solution for your clients. Begin each day by preparing your heart. Also begin each day knowing what your target is and aim beyond that target.

2. PROSPECTING

Work each day to develop effective prospecting skills and habits. The single most important thing about prospecting is that you do it daily. Prospect on an organized, time-protected schedule and in a systematic way. Ask daily who has a want or need for your valuable proposition as well as the authority and budget to buy from you. Make a list of potential prospects and work your list. Keep an audio recorder in your vehicle and, as you travel and notice businesses that may have a need for what you have to offer, record an audio note and add it to your list. Be willing to make the calls most people won't.

Be strategically visible in the media that your target group reads, and at social and civic/community events as an active contributor, not as a function of strategy but as a function of authentic character. Network actively and make yourself useful to others.

Great contacts
bring great contracts.

Proactively engage people in conversation. Refer to a commonly shared reality to establish and maintain rapport.

With telephone prospecting, ask for a 15-minute face-to-face appointment with a pre-qualified prospect if that is feasible. For most prospective clients, do not sell your product or service on the phone, just sell the appointment. You may want to consider hiring an appointment setter to do this for you. Let your positive reputation precede you so that people will long to meet you. Your appointment setter may say, "Hello, my name is________ and I represent one of the top_______ in/at ____________. She/he has asked me to do a quick two or three-question survey. Will you please be so kind as to briefly answer these questions for us?"

3. FACT-FINDING AND HANDLING OBJECTIVE

Be sure you are selling to the decision-makers. Facilitate

them talking to you by first asking for information. Never say something you could ask them to tell you. Seek out their pain, problems and frustrations. Once you begin to understand what it is they need, explore their decision-making criteria and strategy by asking the single most important question in sales, "What do you value the most in_________?" If they have used a similar product or service in the past, ask how they made the purchase decision. What was the process? Understand how they buy.

Proactively, early in the meeting, inoculate them against the most likely one or two objections. State the most likely objection(s) as a reframed positive.

You may find the following word patterns useful:

- "A lot of our most satisfied clients/customers used to be concerned about that until_______"
- "Now just suppose we can do something about________ or add _____________ at little or nor additional cost to you, would you be willing to _________"

See objectives as a natural part of the sales cycle and as a disguised request for more clarifying information, or for more benefits and value so that they can justify the purchase. Test close after handling a major objection, with a friendly, positive question to determine their level of interest.

4. PRESENTATION

Confirm how much time you have beforehand. Build rapport and trust. Make the product or service the star of the presentation and present in a planned, systematic way.

Begin by asking great questions that will engage them. Make your presentation highly interactive. Ask, "How much detail do you want?" Focus on showing the benefits to them based on what they said is most important to them. Use a preponderance of evidence to back your claim.

Use pre-planned questions and impact statements with flexibility in a pre-planned framework. Ask, "If we can show you a way to_______ (state the benefit they most want or need) will you?" Get them to pre-commit to some degree if you can.

Provide them with useful information aligned with what they most value. Become their trusted advisor. Ask appropriate questions and listen more than you speak in your sales presentation. Dare to present with enthusiasm, passion and a touch of animation. Say things in an unusual way and do things in an unusual way to be memorable. Selectively use unusual postures or movement to increase impact. Use positive body language. Handle the product or documentation with great care because it adds to the perceived value.

Keep your presentation brief, yet adequately comprehensive. Show the big picture and details with more emphasis on what *they* said, *they* want, and in what *they* show the most interest. Solve their problem.

With group presentations:

- Be absolutely and totally well-prepared.
- Start with a thought-provoking question, brief impact statement or humorous story. Show an appropriate cartoon or video clip with a message to set the stage.
- Position yourself at the center of your setting and actively involve your audience.

- Maintain good eye contact with all the key decision-makers.
- Make 3 to 7 key points and highlight the most important point with a story. Provide solid take-home value early in the presentation.
- Close with heart and ask for their business, looking directly at the key decision-maker. If the opportunity to do so is pre-agreed upon and scheduled, it may even be more effective to sit one-on-one after the presentation with the key decision maker to close the deal.

5. CLOSING THE SALE

Before you close, it is very effective to amplify their pain by asking, "What will happen if you don't ________?" To set the stage for the close, show them how what you offer will solve their problems and remove their "pain." Whenever appropriate and possible, let them hold, touch, and smell what you sell. Facilitate an experience.

With more complex, big-ticket and intangible offerings, use the "Benjamin Franklin balance sheet close" of listing positives and negatives side-by-side, breaking them down into a cost-benefit analysis with a financial bottom line benefit for them. Use words such as "invest," "acquire," "own" and "authorize," instead of "buy" and "sign."

Before you finally close with a committing question, ask, "Is there anything else that you value, which we haven't discussed yet?"

Assume the sale and close boldly. Remain silent after asking your final closing question. Wait for the answer. Do not sell beyond the sale.

6. ENSURE REFERRALS AND FOLLOW-UP

To get referrals, do an awesome job and then ask for them. Be specific. Prompt their mind with soft, gentle questions. Ask for a "back-of-their-business-card" endorsement. Use it as an entry ticket/discussion starter when you meet the lead given to you. Follow up on all leads as well as all past clients/customers. Week 1, call all the A, B & C's; week 2 call all the D, E & F's etc. Be systematic.

Any hope or dream of yours is unattainable unless you personally do something about it.

With Walk-in Retail Sales

1. Smile warm and deep.
2. Greet in a friendly, open and respectful manner.
3. Maintain a respectful distance.
4. Use open body postures.
5. Be available and attentive.
6. Establish their need(s) with a few great questions.
7. Help them get what they want and need.

Shine as a Customer-Care Ambassador

1. Smile and greet people in a friendly manner.
2. Listen attentively.
3. Edify and acknowledge them.
4. Manage the memory of the experience with good-will gestures.
5. Go the extra mile in what they most value.
6. Keep them informed of progress.
7. Give something extra to keep them as a customer.

With Network Marketing:

1. Be a passionate user of the product and where appropriate, use it publicly and share it with others.
2. Work on your own personal growth daily.
3. Develop dynamic people and leadership skills.
4. Network actively and develop leaders who can duplicate the system.
5. Focus on helping ever-increasing numbers of people get to the next level.
6. Always take new people to each major training meeting.
7. Persist, show the plan, and demonstrate the product daily.

Give it at least three to seven years of dedication and the results will delight you.

Chapter 12

Live Generously and Retire Comfortably

Do you sometimes wonder whether you are making the most that you can of your life and money? If so, I have included a few tips you may wish to consider.

I have been incredibly fortunate for many years now to meet some of the most successful people in the world today. I offer you a brief summary of some of the most valuable key points I have been privileged to learn from these rich and famous people on a one-on-one basis. Here are some of the fundamentals I have learned and what I believe.

> "Live life to make a difference not just a profit; but do make a great profit so that you can make a greater difference in the lives of ever-growing numbers of people."

"From those to whom much is given, much is expected."

"You have not yet lived a perfect day until you have helped someone in need who will never be able to repay your kindness."

"We can't close our eyes to all the suffering in this world. If you can't feed many, at least feed one."

Here is what you can do to build a more secure future in business:

- Have a clear vision and mission.
- Believe that if you show what you have to enough people, someone will buy.
- Be totally honest.
- Focus on a limited number of future goals.
- Raise your standards.
- Build networks.
- Go for volume.
- Ask, "What is your opinion?"
- Think cash flow and systems.
- Operate as a team; ensure role clarity.
- Find a need and fill it.
- Help others to make money from what you do/offer.
- Provide quality at a fair price.
- Be opportunity minded.
- Dare to be different—have a unique offering.
- Drive sales, think distribution and duplication.
- Provide an outstanding customer experience with something extra.
- Demonstrate respect, appreciation and gratitude.

- Act boldly with faith, passion and enthusiasm.
- Always leave a fair profit margin for the next person on the table. Greed and fear are both killers of good deals.
- Encourage and support solid family values

TIPS FOR SUCCESS IN REAL ESTATE

Here is what I have learned from my mentors and personal exposure and work with such people as Robert Kiyosaki of *Rich Dad, Poor Dad* fame.

- The goal is to have adequate real estate and/or a big enough networking downline in place to ensure a monthly passive and/or residual cash flow that is greater than your total expenses.

- Invest for returns, not appreciation. See appreciation as a bonus. Acquire mostly smaller units in good areas. Build a portfolio of multiple units for ever-growing cash flow.

- Do not buy overvalued properties in an overheated market; instead, wait and buy selectively during real estate market slumps and crashes, and sell your weak performers when everyone else is buying.

- Do your homework, do your own detailed research, choose an area and become the most knowledgeable assessor of need and market value in that area. Keep a journal with values and continually make value comparisons. There is always a great deal out there somewhere. Look for value, know the market, and be the authority on what the values are.

- Use leverage. Real estate offers an outstanding opportunity to leverage investment funds as it enables the investor to take control of an appreciating asset at a small percentage of the asset's overall value, and to use time and inflation as leveraging tools in servicing the debt with potentially depreciating currency.

All across the world, wealthy people use real estate as their primary vehicle for wealth enhancement within a balanced and diversified investment portfolio. A small but growing portfolio of rental units can be an ideal part-time business to get one into earning passive income while still building a corporate career.

Real estate, although slower to convert to money than other investments and in spite of occasional tenant challenges, remains a fantastic investment. It serves a foundational human need and is an effective long-term hedge against inflation.

I believe that real estate is one of the finest vehicles for turning a portion of one's earned income into passive income. It allows you not only to use your own money, but also your banker's money, to invest in appreciated assets that can generate dependable, positive cash flow while it appreciates in value for later capital gains.

Warning: using too much of your banker's money can also create massive pain if used incorrectly and irresponsibly.

With Real Estate, look for:

1. The right market segment
   The segment where most people are able to buy or rent in. Look for a future high demand area. Remember the mantras of location, location, location and cash flow, cash flow, cash flow.

2. The right seller
   Distressed, motivated, flexible.
   Ask, "Why are you/they selling?

3. Distressed properties
   Structurally sound, in need of cosmetic attention, where the total renovation cost will not exceed more than 15% of the end value. They usually can be acquired below market value.
   Inspect surrounding ground for clay, cracked walls. Inspect the roof, security systems, communication systems, water systems, and electrical systems. Look for dampness, termites, environmental pollution, and neighborhood realities, etc.
   Do a complete and accurate inspection always.

4. Conversion opportunities
   Take a picture, and as you look at it ask, "What can this become for which there is a need"?
   Can it be rezoned?
   What will its maximum value use be?
   Research the title, zoning, appraised value, comparative properties, restrictions, taxes, liens, etc.

5. Favorable Terms & Conditions
   Ask, "Would you take_____" type questions
   Sign as______/or nominee/assigns as______, and subject

to____________and a due diligence period of___ business days

6. Cash flow and capital gains potential
   Invest predominantly for cash flow; see capital gains as a bonus.
   To lease right and eventually to sell right you have to first buy right.
   Look at many properties and then narrow it down to buy one.
   How can you optimize your profits?

Work the numbers, do the numbers behind the numbers, and be sure that the numbers work out for all concerned. Invest in assets that provide a positive cash flow.

Financing Your Deals

Ask yourself, "How can I do this without money, at least without any of my own money, or with the least amount of money down?"

As a general rule, banks everywhere are eager to finance good applications; the key is to make yourself a good applicant.

Banks look at key factors such as applicants' reliability and trustworthiness based on track record, credit history, net worth, ability to repay (income) and other factors such as what security exists for the loan, as well as the prevailing and forecasted economic market conditions.

When using your banker's money to invest in real estate, it is wise not to overstretch or overcommit yourself. When hard economic times come around, as they predictably do, interest rates will rise and tenant defaults will increase, putting landlords under pressure.

The secret is to build profitable businesses and to let your businesses acquire real estate with pre-tax income, and turn each of your real estate units into profitable businesses.

Key Actions
1. Educate yourself financially.
2. Build a relationship with your banker(s).
3. Build collateral and an advisory team; be sure to include a banker, accountant, mortgage consultant, attorney, realtor and a seasoned real estate investor.
4. Be organized and professional.
5. Leave an up-to-date paper trail. Put everything in writing, think preponderance of proof as in legal evidence.

Typically for mortgage applications, the minimum documentation required will be:

1. Identification document(s)
2. Social Security number
3. Proof of income, e.g. recent paycheck stubs
4. Bank statements for the preceding three to six months
5. List of creditors.

A legal entity will need:
1. Trust or corporation documents
2. Up-to-date financial statements
3. Bank statements in the name of the legal entity for the proceeding three to six months

4. A resolution that authorizes the purchase
5. List of creditors

A few words of advice:

1. Establish yourself as a credible client and especially as an industrious commercial borrower with two or more banks.
2. Pay all your debt on time. Ideally, pay a little extra each time and keep a comprehensive record of proof in a totally safe place with a back up in a second location.
3. Build up a fund of saved cash on hand.
4. Investigate buying and owning each investment real estate unit or development in a separate land trust.

What to do if your mortgage application is declined:

As a former shareholder in a busy mortgage organization firm, I learned that it is absolutely possible for a perfectly good application to be declined due to human error in data capture and processing. If your application is ever declined, find out exactly why. Be suspicious of errors on your credit report, miscalculations, incorrect data capture and/or incorrect credit checks. Have it re-checked and consider another lending institution.

How to Make Money With Real Estate

1. Purchase well-located, below market value units.
2. Invest to build a rental portfolio. For passive, positive cash flow, see capital gains as a bonus.
3. Sell only when everyone is buying and then only sell

your worst performers or units in an area that is about to change negatively.
4. “Flip” very selectively. Yes, you can make money with speculation, but I believe it is wise to build an ever-growing rental unit portfolio as your primary strategy.

There is a belief among experienced landlords that the right unit attracts and keeps the right tenant(s). You will be well-positioned if:

1. Your rental unit(s) are located in a moderate-income, peaceful, predominantly owner-occupied area...

2. ...where mostly middle-class, working (employed), church going, family people with children live.

3. If the unit(s) are close to good schools, popular churches, reasonably upscale shopping centers/malls, hospitals/medical centers, good employment opportunities, fitness, sports and recreation facilities, especially clean natural open space conservation areas...

4. ...have access to good public transportation routes as well as a high-speed internet lines and good security, you will be well positioned to attract good tenants.

Use a contract that is totally fair. Protect your interest without exploiting. Secure a 1-1/2 to 2 month deposit up-front. Place the full deposit in a trust account, give proof to the tenant and give the tenant all interest earned, upon termination of the lease.

Make your policies, rules and expectations very clear and

give them in writing. Specify that the tenants are responsible for all minor maintenance and that a late payment penalty applies. Insist that your tenants pay their rent with an automatic bank draft.

As for your primary residence, we recommend you purchase your dream home during a market crash slump. Look for an older home you can remodel to your specifications in an older, well-established upper middle class area, in a mid-price range.

Note: Research "tax-deferred exchanges" as a strategy for buying and selling real estate in a way that allows you to legally defer payment on your capital gains profit (Section 1031, Internal Revenue Code).

Stocks

The stock market can be a tricky place in which to invest. The following tips will help you with your future stock market considerations:

1. Educate yourself: observe, study, read, learn, join an investment club/network and attend reputable seminars and workshops. Build superior and specialized knowledge. Remain current and informed.

2. Always invest based on the real value of the company behind the stocks, not so much whether the market is going up or down. Do your own due diligence.

3. Build a team of advisors and do your own detailed and accurate research.

4. Invest intelligently not emotionally. Do not let other peoples' hype, perceptions, opinions, greed and/or fear drive your decisions. Be in control and take full responsibility for your own decisions and results.

5. Be willing to be different. Dare to go the opposite way from the crowds.

6. Only invest as much as you can comfortably afford to lose.

Above all, do not let your focus just be on making money. Focus on building businesses that serve a real and growing need; and, always remember it is wise to make one's priorities God, family, business, community and, only then, yourself. Don't just make money; make a difference and fulfill your purpose. Let money be a by-product but not an all-consuming obsession.

THE DAILY SEVEN LIFE-BUILDER LOG*

Week ______________ Day ____________ Date________

Start time/planned activity — End time/actual activity

1. Spiritual Enrichment

______________________ ______________________

______________________ ______________________

______________________ ______________________

2. Mental Development

______________________ ______________________

______________________ ______________________

______________________ ______________________

3. Physical Conditioning

______________________ ______________________

______________________ ______________________

______________________ ______________________

4. Intelligent Nutrition

______________________ ______________________

______________________ ______________________

______________________ ______________________

5. Purpose Fulfillment

______________________ ______________________

______________________ ______________________

______________________ ______________________

6. Family Time

______________________ ______________________

______________________ ______________________

______________________ ______________________

7. Quiet Time

______________________ ______________________

______________________ ______________________

______________________ ______________________

*To help you track your progress, copy and use this form as needed.

The Daily Seven Experience

Discover new distinctions and deeper understanding of The Daily Seven life-management system live with David Fabricius or one of his certified and licensed facilitators. Come and live the experiences at one of our Daily Seven Retreats. Bring a friend, you will benefit tremendously.

For further information please visit
www.heartwaregroup.com
www.davidfabricius.com and/or www.TheDailySeven.com

Products & Services

To view and acquire available products and services please visit us at www.davidfabricius.com

Afterword

Congratulations! If you read the entire book you are a very special kind of person and clearly possess the drive, hunger and persistence to achieve your goals. I respect you, for it is not just anyone who will do what you have just done. I encourage you to go forth and take your place among the great ones in your chosen industry, community and nation because you can! Do not settle for less. Step up and fulfill your purpose gloriously and leave the world a little better off because you did what you came to do and did it in outstanding excellence for the glory of God!

About the Author

David Fabricius is an internationally known keynote speaker, team builder, spiritual retreat leader and trainer with strong crossover appeal, having reached both very large secular and religious audiences across many cultures and denominations worldwide.

By the gift and grace of God, David has touched and enriched the lives of people from more than a hundred nations across five continents, and his contribution is growing.

His mission is to help millions of business people to discover their life purpose revealed through a personal relationship with God and to enjoy the authentic confidence to go for it, without destroying or losing their health, family or soul for the sake of another position, award or dollar.

In corporations he teach leadership, sales, customer care and life/time management. His clients includes Microsoft, Lucent Technologies, Lexmark, Ford Motor Company, Xerox, PriceWaterhouseCoopers, Alexander Forbes, YPO, RE/MAX and many other outstanding organizations from virtually every major industry.

David's slogan is not just words. Much as he loves words he encourages people to be doers of the Word and as a faith-filled believer includes highly memorable metaphors as a way to educate and entertain.

David Fabricius is now ready to facilitate, accelerate and celebrate your and your team/organizations success. He is available for convention keynotes, private teachings, self-esteem and team-building experiences and specialized/customized leadership, time/life-management, sales and customer care training sessions. At corporate and association meetings David remain very careful, respectful and professional not to include religion unless it is authorized by the major shareholders and most senior leadership.

If you beyond a shadow of a doubt can honestly say you benefited from reading *THE DAILY SEVEN*, we will appreciate you giving a copy of this book to everyone in your circle of influence and look forward to presenting a special tailor-made seminar for your entire organization, group or team, or to at least meet you in person at one of our public seminars and hear how you live The Daily Seven.

We would like to include your inspiring story in a follow-up book titled *Living THE DAILY SEVEN*. In it will be stories that touch, inspire and compel. Can you imagine your story being the one most readers can relate to? Your example could inspire them to explore a closer personal relationship with God, find their purpose and bring a breakthrough solution to the market that will solve a real problem for millions of people globally.

What People Are Saying About David Fabricius:

"David Fabricius made a tremendous impact on our members. His teachings are thought provoking, motivating and challenging; in fact, he enabled us to perform feats most of us did not think possible. He has an amazing ability to infuse and inspire people. Our London chapter is a very demanding audience with the highest standards. The rating given to our event with David was 9.7, with the majority of members rating David's presentation 10/10. It is an event that we will never forget. We highly recommend David Fabricius as an excellent resource."

—Karan F. Billimoria, CBE, DLMA Law (Cambridge), London, England

David Fabricius understands the rewards of success and the exhilaration that comes from being outstanding in one's field. He also knows the cost to the human soul that ruthless pursuit of excellence can exact. High achievers will find THE DAILY SEVEN both an inspiring and practical guide for re-orienting themselves to what really counts in this world and learning to live a grounded, balanced life. The practices that David teaches enable us to enjoy our success without losing our humanity. The world desperately needs leaders who achieve great things, while remaining authentic human beings.

—Helen H. Hand, Ph.D., Licensed Clinical Psychologist and President of Colorado Free University, Denver, Colorado

"David Fabricius' Daily Seven provided us with a practical, doable roadmap that changed the lives of our whole group."

—Steve Harvey, Managing Director, Dakota Capital, Dallas, Texas

"David Fabricius gets to the core of what really matters; it does not get any better than this. David opened my mind to a whole new world of thinking."

—Professor Jeannie Kahwajy, PhD, Stanford University

MBA Program Director, International Institute for Management Development, Lausanne, Switzerland

"From someone who has seen it all, awesome, powerful, extraordinary." —Michelle Lemmons-Poscente, President, International Speakers Bureau, Dallas, Texas

"We saw measurable results and a sales record within the first 7 days. Our sales more than doubled in 5 weeks and grew by 300% in 50 days."
—Tom Krulis, Managing Director, Godfreys, Melbourne, Australia.

"David will help you in ways you can only imagine."
—Grant D. Fraser, CLU, ChFC, President, Fraser Financial Group, Los Angeles, California

"David's earthquake of a presentation shook the very foundation of our business, exposing its cracks and weaknesses. Once repaired, the company was able to unleash explosive growth in sales." —Mark Layton, Chairman & CEO, PFSweb, Dallas, Texas

"Extraordinary, talented and thought-provoking. David Fabricius knows how to develop people beyond their comfort zones." —Professor Jacques Horovitz, PhD, Columbia University, Director-Executive Education, International Institute for Management Development (IMD), Lausanne, Switzerland.

"David Fabricius is an outstanding business educator. He has an extraordinary ability to educate, inspire and unify people at all levels." —Professor N.G. Beard, Oxford University Alumni, Life Fellow of the Royal Society of Arts, Academic Director ICESA Management and Leadership Academy, Cambridge University Partner, Durban, South Africa.

"David is one of the most effective communicators I have ever seen." —Professor Marc Badoux, Swiss Federal Institute of Technology, Lausanne, Switzerland.

"David helps others to bring their light to the world and positively impacts the great cities on the edges of the earth."
—Evangelist Jarrod Davidoff, Founder and President, Save the World Foundation, Orlando, Florida

"David's' teaching are thought provoking, powerful and create real lasting value in peoples lives... irrespective of their culture, personal background, race or gender."
—Willie Linssen, Professor, Seoul School of Integrated Sciences & Technologies, Seoul, South Korea